PETER C. DOOLEY

introductory
macroeconomic

introductory
macroeconomics

introductory macroeconomics

PETER C. DOOLEY
University of Saskatchewan

RANDOM HOUSE NEW YORK

To JOHN WARREN DOOLEY

First Edition

987654321

Copyright © 1975 by Random House, Inc.
All rights reserved under International and Pan-American
Copyright Conventions. No part of this book may be
reproduced in any form or by any means, electronic or
mechanical, including photocopying, without permission in
writing from the publisher. All inquiries should be addressed
to Random House, Inc., 201 East 50th Street, New York, N.Y.
10022. Published in the United States by Random House, Inc.,
and simultaneously in Canada by Random House of
Canada Limited, Toronto.

Library of Congress Cataloging in Publication Data

Dooley, Peter C
    Introductory macroeconomics.
    Includes bibliographical references.
    1. Macroeconomics. I. Title.
HB171.5.D617   339   74-9957
ISBN 0-394-31757-2

MANUFACTURED IN THE UNITED STATES OF AMERICA

Design by Marsha Picker

Cover by Arthur D. Ritter

CONTENTS

introductory macroeconomics

INTRODUCTION

Economics Defined

The economic organization of society involves the production and consumption of goods and services. Whether men live in a primitive tribe or in a modern nation state, economic activity is essential to life and is a large part of life. Food, clothing, and shelter do not come to us like manna from heaven. They are scarce relative to the needs of mankind, and they require the sacrifice of labor and time to acquire. Scarcity exists and scarcity is the essence of all economic problems.

Economics is the study of the allocation of resources among competing uses. The uses of time, labor services, and raw materials are practically endless, but the available amounts of these resources are limited. It is not possible to satisfy people's every desire. If everyone wanted to live in a mansion, eat lobster, drink champagne, and be served by a butler, a cook, and a maid, everyone would have to be rich, a lobsterman, a vintager, a butler, a cook, and a maid all at once. Scarcity limits what can be done and makes choices necessary, both for the individual and for society.

Microeconomics explains the choices made by individual consumers and producers. It is based on the theory of consumer behavior, which analyzes the market transactions of the individual household, and on the theory of the firm, which examines the profit-making activities of the individual business enterprise. With these theories of individual behavior as its foundation, microeconomics explains how the relative prices of goods and services allocate resources among competing uses—how, for example, the high price of platinum relative to iron allocates each metal to different uses.

Macroeconomics explains the behavior of aggregate groups of transactors. Instead of exploring how the individual household spends its income or how an enterprise runs its business, macroeconomics simplifies reality by collecting like transactors into aggregate groups. It treats all consumers as a group, all corporations as a group, all laborers as a group, and so on. Each aggregate group is assumed to act as if it were a unit. Also, instead of investigating all the thousands of different markets in the economy, it collects like transactions into aggregates, such as the total expenditures by consumers on goods and services or the total amount of labor employed in the economy.

The distinction between microeconomics and macroeconomics is, to a certain extent, artificial. Both are based on the same fundamental principles, for the individual units of microeconomics can be added up to form the aggregate groups of macroeconomics; but the behavior of the aggregates poses problems that are different from the behavior of the individual parts. Microeconomics explains why the price of beef is high relative to the price of bread or why doctors are better paid than nurses, whereas macroeconomics examines why all prices are rising or why national income is falling.

Macroeconomics developed historically to explain the functiong of the national economy and to guide the policy makers of the national government. It can be applied to smaller or larger political and geographical units, such as the state of California or the European Common Market, but it has generally been applied to the economic activities of the nation state, because national governments are responsible for dealing with basic macroeconomic problems such as unemployment and inflation.

Three Macroeconomic Problems

This book is concerned with three macroeconomic problems: unemployment, inflation, and balance-of-payments disequilibrium. All three are short-term problems that can quickly develop into major political and economic crises, crises that divert the attention of the government from such fundamental and long-term issues as the rate of economic growth, the distribution of income among the population, and the preservation of the natural environment. All three problems must be treated together, because the effectiveness of the policy used to combat any one of them depends on the policy used to combat the others. The cure for one is often the cause of another.

Unemployment is defined in economic theory as existing when people who are willing to work at the going wage are unable to find work. Since they are unemployed against their will, they are said to be involuntarily unemployed. They are forced to live off their savings or go on relief. People who prefer not to work at the going wage—perhaps because they are retired, in school, or housewives—are not involuntarily unemployed and are not counted among the unemployed.

Unemployment has been perhaps the most serious economic problem for industrial countries in the twentieth century. Unemployment makes both the individual and society worse off than they would be if everyone who wanted to work could find a job. The unemployed individual is poorer and frequently suffers psychologically, especially in a society that considers work a virtue and unemployment a disgrace. The society is poorer as well, because fewer goods and services are produced when part of the labor force is not at work.

Inflation is defined as a persistent rise in the average level of prices. Inflation is measured by the prices of goods and services and not by the incomes of laborers, capitalists, and landlords, since incomes rise because of improved productivity as well as inflationary pressures. *Productivity* is measured by output per man, per machine, or per acre. An increase in output per man, per machine, or per acre due to technological change may permit prices to fall while incomes rise. For example, a farmer's income may rise over time as the number of acres he works increases or as the yield per acre increases, even though the price of farm products may fall. A fall in the average level of prices is called *deflation*.

Inflation is a social problem because it tends to redistribute income, making some people richer and other people poorer. People who live on fixed incomes, such as pensioners, suffer a loss in welfare because the quantity of goods and services that they can buy with their fixed money incomes declines as the prices of goods and services rise. Their real income declines. *Real income* is measured by money income divided by the average level of prices. It is sometimes called *deflated income*. While people on fixed money incomes lose, other people gain from inflation; for, it stands to reason, if one group can buy only a smaller share of a given volume of output, some other group must be able to buy a larger share of that output. Those laborers and businessmen whose wages and profits rise more rapidly during periods of inflation than during periods of stable prices gain what pensioners and others lose. Real estate speculators, for example, often gain during periods of inflation.

A *balance-of-payments disequilibrium* occurs when the amount that one country spends abroad tends not to equal the amount that other countries spend in that country. The amount that a country spends abroad is made up of a variety of items: imports of goods and services, such as foreign cars and foreign travel; transfer payments, such as gifts to relatives abroad and aid to foreign governments; and financial transactions, such as lending to a foreign country and investing in a foreign corporation. When the amount that is sent abroad for such items does not equal the amount that is received, the difference is measured by a balance-of-payments surplus or deficit—a surplus when receipts exceed expenditures, a deficit when the outflow exceeds the inflow.

Balance-of-payments surpluses and deficits have been settled historically by building up or drawing down the international reserves of a country. In the nineteenth century gold was the primary international reserve; today it is U. S. dollars, although other currencies and other financial arrangements are also used. A balance-of-payments deficit tends to draw down reserves, while a surplus tends to increase reserves.

A balance-of-payments disequilibrium becomes a social problem when it is substantial and persistent. Minor fluctuations in international reserves about a safe level occur all the time and do not require a change in a nation's economic policies. A substantial and persistent disequilibrium, however, may require a government to pursue policies that either alter the volume of domestic production or switch expenditures between foreign and domestic products. In either event, the economic well-being of the population is affected.

The Circular Flow Diagram

A national economy is too complex to be treated in detail. Simplification is necessary, for it is not possible to comprehend everything at once. A large corporation, for example, transacts in many different markets. It hires many types of labor—janitors, machinists, truckers, electricians, secretaries, salesmen, lawyers, accountants, and so on—each of which is subdivided into various grades and descriptions. At the same time, a large corporation may buy and sell products as different as locomotives and paper clips. In addition to large corporations, there are smaller businesses, households, and governmental and foreign transactors in the economy. Macroeconomics deals with this complexity by treating broad groups of transactors, such as all producers, as if they were a single transactor, and by treating similar transactions, such as purchases of newly produced goods and services, as if they were one.

Figure 0–1 is a circular flow diagram that presents a highly aggregative view of the economy. It traces the flow of goods and services between two major groups of transactors: producers and purchasers—those who make and those who buy all the goods and services produced in the economy. The total of goods and services produced in the economy within a given period of time is called current production, or output. The distinction between a producer and a purchaser of output is func-

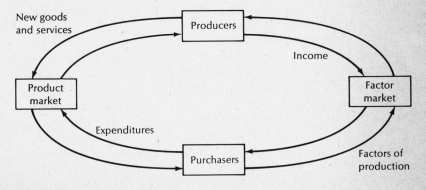

Figure 0-1   Circular Flow Diagram

tional by type of transaction, not by type of transactor, because many individuals both produce and purchase output. A farmer, for example, is a producer when he is selling his crop, but he is a purchaser when he is buying a steak or a tractor. His functions as a producer and as a purchaser are as conceptually distinct from each other as growing a tomato is distinct from eating it. When he consumes his own production, he is treated in Figure 0–1 as if he sold part of his production to his own household.

Producers create new goods and services with the factors of production, which are traditionally classified as land, labor, and capital. Figure 0–1 simplifies the complex nature of transactions between producers and purchasers by assuming that the producing sector buys only the factors of production and sells only finished goods and services to their final purchasers. Purchasers buy current production with the income they receive from selling their labor services, renting their land, and advancing their capital to producers.

Producers and purchasers face each other in two different markets: the *product* market and the *factor* market. Producers *supply* and purchasers *demand* new goods and services in the product market, where current production, or output, is exchanged for dollars. Producers demand and purchasers supply the services of land, labor, and capital in the factor market, where factor services are exchanged for money income. Figure 0–1 shows two flows of equal value that move in opposite directions. The outer arrows show the direction of the flow of goods and services, that is, factor services and current production. The inner arrows indicate the flow of funds that pays for factor services and current production. In the marketplace, current production is equal in value to the expenditure of funds on it. The expenditures that purchasers make in the product market equal the income that they receive in the factor market. Every dollar spent is a dollar received.

The purchasing sector of the economy can be divided into four subsectors, which are identified by the type of current production they purchase: consumer goods, capital goods, government services, and exports minus imports. Exports minus imports measures that portion of our production purchased by the rest of the world less what we purchase abroad. The rest of the world includes all the countries with which we trade, treated as an aggregate group. These four types of goods and services are called the components of *aggregate demand;* and the four purchasing subsectors are called *households, investors, government,* and the *rest of the world.*

Organization of the Book

This book develops the theoretical tools needed to analyze three macroeconomic problems: unemployment, inflation, and balance-of-payments disequilibrium. Like the abstract concept of the circular flow of goods and services, theoretical tools simplify reality. They provide a framework in which facts can be arranged, and they describe the way in which one set of facts relates to another. Without this collection of hypotheses, which we call macroeconomic theory, the three problems under consideration could not even be defined, much less measured, analyzed, and corrected.

Chapter 1, which introduces some essential concepts, is really microeconomics. It describes the principles that govern the behavior of individual decision-making units, especially households and business enterprises. Chapter 2 on private and social accounting shows how individual microeconomic units are aggregated and provides a framework that relates one macroeconomic unit to another. Chapters 3 through 6 analyze the behavior of the four macroeconomic purchasing subsectors: households, investors, government, and the rest of the world. With the exception of the government, which is assumed to act for political reasons that transcend narrow economic motives, the purchasing subsectors behave according to the principles discussed in Chapter 1. The aggregate demand of these four purchasers directly determines the amount of current production and national income and indirectly affects the volume of employment, the level of prices, and the balance of international trade. The theory is not complete, however, without Chapter 7, on money and interest, because financial markets influence the behavior of the purchasing subsectors and are in turn influenced by them. Our three critical problems are discussed in the last chapters: unemployment in Chapter 8, inflation in Chapter 9, and balance-of-payments disequilibrium in Chapter 10.

SOME
ESSENTIAL
CONCEPTS

Economic analysis explains how people allocate scarce resources among competing uses. Without scarcity, there would be no economic problem and no economic analysis. People could acquire as much of anything as they desired. Everything would be free. With scarcity, people must economize in their use of time and resources in order to obtain the greatest benefit for the least sacrifice. Economic behavior is often referred to as maximizing behavior, because people tend to choose the best of alternative benefits or, what amounts to the same thing, the least of alternative sacrifices.

Economic analysis presupposes that scarcity exists and that people try to maximize their material well-being. Taking scarcity and maximizing behavior as its basic assumptions, economic analysis builds on four fundamental concepts: the principle of opportunity cost, the subjective nature of household preferences, the technical organization of production, and equilibrium. Transactors use the principle of opportunity cost to calculate their advantage in supplying and demanding goods and services; subjective preferences of households underlie the demand for output and the supply of factor services; technical relations of production underlie the supply of output and the demand for factor services by productive enterprises; and the supply and demand for goods and services tend to an equilibrium .in the market. While these theoretical tools may appear far removed from practical affairs, the analysis of actual economic problems generally involves the use of one or more of them.

Opportunity Cost

The *principle of opportunity cost* is used to measure the cost of a course of action. As long as we live in a world where time and resources are limited but where alternative uses of time and resources are virtually unlimited, scarcity exists and choices are necessary. All things cannot be done at the same time, and all possible goods cannot be produced from available resources. When one course of action is taken, other opportunities are foregone.

The principle of opportunity cost states: *The cost of doing one thing is measured by comparing it with the cost of the next best opportunity foregone.*

Each opportunity must be compared to its nearest alternative in order to make a rational choice. For example, the cost of a college education is not just the cost of books, tuition, and fees; it also includes the cost of opportunities foregone. If a student could earn $10,000 a year instead of going to school, the immediate cost of his education is at least $10,000 a year, even if a scholarship pays his way. While he is in school, he is sacrificing $10,000 a year in income. That sacrifice measures the real cost of his education. However, if he expects to earn more income over his lifetime or lead a fuller life as the result of his education, the advantage may well lie on the side of the temporary sacrifice.

Economic behavior in its most elementary form involves calculating the cost of alternatives and choosing that alternative which offers the greatest reward or least sacrifice. In economic analysis, a consumer is assumed to choose that combination of goods which he most prefers, given his income and the prices he must pay; a laborer is assumed to choose that occupation and that amount of work which he most prefers, given the opportunity cost, the subjective nature of household preferences, produce that volume of output and hire that quantity of labor which is expected to maximize its profits.

The principle of opportunity cost is a guide to future action, a planning tool, which applies whether the choice involves an objective comparison in money terms, as in the case of the corporation, or a subjective evaluation of individual preferences, as in the case of the consumer or laborer. Choice among alternative courses of action is necessarily based on expectations, which may not ultimately be realized, since the future can not be known with certainty. Times change and unforeseen events occur so that the household and corporation may both ultimately be disappointed when their plans do not turn out as expected. The economic activity of both individual and corporate transactors is governed by their expectations.

Household Preferences

Individual preferences lie behind the choices that households make in the consumer goods, labor, financial, and other markets. These preferences are subjective and differ from one person to another. Since the social, physiological, and psychological elements that determine individual preferences do not change rapidly over time, they can be taken as given and the individual assumed to arrange his transactions in the goods, services, and financial markets so that he maximizes his well-being. He chooses those alternatives which he most prefers, whether that means buying a sports car, becoming a musician, or entering the clergy.

Each household faces a budget constraint. It is constrained by the amount of its money income and by the prices it must pay for goods and services in the market. When these constraints change, the quantities of goods and services purchased or sold by individuals change, even though subjective preferences remain the same. The effect of changes in money income and the effect of changes in market prices on household transactions are considered in turn.

Changes in Money Income   As the money income of a household increases, it will ordinarily increase its consumption expenditures; similarly, it will ordinarily reduce its total expenditures if its money income falls. What is true of total expenditures, however, need not be true of all the component parts, because a consumer who expects his income to rise may prefer to increase the quality as well as the quantity of the goods he consumes. A consumer may want to buy some new luxury good that he has never purchased before when income increases and, at the same time, buy less of some other good that he thinks is of inferior quality.

Three possibilities exist. First, the quantity purchased of an *ordinary good* increases as money income increases, assuming market prices do not change. Most goods are ordinary goods. Second, the quantity of an *inferior good* purchased decreases as money income increases, again assuming that prices remain unchanged. Third, the quantity purchased of a *neutral good* does not change as money income changes.

Examples of an ordinary good (beef) and an inferior good (bread) are shown in Table 1–1. A hypothetical family with only $5,000 a year in income chooses to consume 600 loaves of bread a year but only 100 pounds of beef. The same family or another family with the same preferences would plan to reduce their bread consumption to 400 loaves a year and increase their consumption of beef to 150 pounds a year if they expected their income to be $10,000 a year. As income rises further, less bread and more beef is purchased.

The data in Table 1–1 appear in graphic form in Figure 1–1. The lines connecting the points of planned consumption are called *Engel curves*, named after the nineteenth-century German statistician Ernst Engel. The curves are drawn as if consumption varied continuously with money income, even though only a few points are listed in Table 1–1. The graphs show that the consumption of the ordinary good rises and that the consumption of the inferior good falls as money income increases.

Changes in Market Prices   The effect of price changes on household transactions can be divided into two typical cases: first, the

Table 1-1   Ordinary and Inferior Goods

MONEY INCOME (dollars per year)	QUANTITY OF BEEF (pounds per year)	QUANTITY OF BREAD (loaves per year)
5,000	100	600
10,000	150	400
15,000	200	250
20,000	250	150
25,000	300	100

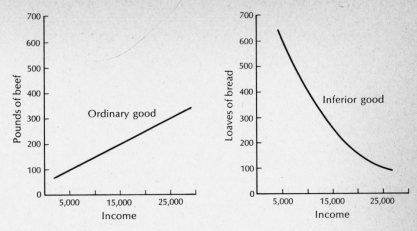

Figure 1-1 Engel Curves for an Ordinary and an Inferior Good

case of consumer demand, where the household is a buyer; second, the case of labor supply, where the household is a seller. While the principles on which these two cases are based are essentially the same, each case is best treated separately.

In the case of consumer demand, an increase in the price of a commodity will usually induce a consumer to demand a smaller quantity of that commodity, provided his money income and other prices remain the same. This is called the *law of demand*. If money income were to change at the same time or if the prices of other commodities were to change, the effect of the change in price of the commodity under consideration would be lost in a crosscurrent of conflicting forces. Provided everything else remains unchanged, however, the quantity demanded of a particular good over a given period of time will generally follow the law of demand.

The law of demand is stated as follows: *The higher the price, the smaller is the quantity demanded; the lower the price, the greater is the quantity demanded.* This definition assumes other factors that affect demand remain unchanged.

The law of demand is illustrated in Table 1–2, where the quantity of bread demanded per year increases as the price of bread falls. If the price were 60 cents a loaf, our hypothetical consumer would want to buy only 40 loaves a year. At 50 cents a loaf, however, he would increase his spending plans to 60 loaves a year. If prices fell still further, still more would be demanded.

Figure 1–2 is a graph of the data in Table 1–2; and, as in the previous graphs, it assumes a continuous relation be-

Table 1-2   The Law of Demand

PRICE (cents per loaf)	QUANTITY DEMANDED (loaves of bread per year)
60	40
50	60
40	100
30	180
20	320
10	640

tween the two variables.[1] The demand curve for bread declines to the right as price falls; this indicates that the lower the price, the greater the quantity demanded. The slope of the curve is negative because of the law of demand; however, whether the curve is concave, convex, or linear depends on the preferences of the individual. In this example it is convex to the origin.

The *elasticity* of demand measures the responsiveness of the quantity demanded to a change in price. It measures whether the quantity demanded changes more than in proportion, less than in proportion, or in the same proportion as a change in the price. It can be calculated by dividing the per-

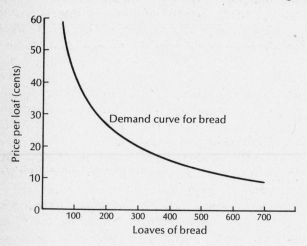

Figure 1-2   The Law of Demand

[1] Contrary to mathematical convention, economists place price, the independent variable, on the vertical instead of the horizontal axis. All the diagrams in this book follow the practice of economists.

centage change in quantity by the percentage change in price.[2] If the quantity demanded rises by 5 percent when the price falls by 1 percent, the demand curve is said to be *elastic*; if the quantity demanded rises by 1 percent because of a 1 percent fall in price, the elasticity of demand is *unitary*; and if the quantity demanded rises by less than 1 percent in response to a 1 percent fall in price, the demand curve is said to be *inelastic*.

In Table 1–2 and in Figure 1–2, when the price of bread falls by one-half from 60 cents to 30 cents a loaf, the quantity demanded rises more than fourfold, from 40 to 180 loaves per year, so that the demand curve is elastic over that range of prices—the quantity demanded changes proportionately more than the price. However, when the price falls by one-half from 20 cents to 10 cents, the quantity demanded merely doubles from 320 to 640 loaves. Since the quantity demanded rises in the same proportion as the price falls over this range of prices, the demand curve is unitarily elastic. As one moves along a demand curve, the elasticity of demand often changes.

The law of demand applies to most goods, but not to all goods. When the price of a good falls and becomes relatively cheaper, a consumer will tend to substitute this cheaper good for other goods, provided his income does not change. This is called the *substitution effect*: A fall in the price of one good relative to the price of a second good will induce a consumer to buy a larger quantity of the first good, provided his income remains unchanged. When the price of a good falls, however, the

---

[2] Elasticity can be calculated from the following formula:

$$\text{elasticity} = \frac{Q_1 - Q_2}{Q_1 + Q_2} \bigg/ \frac{P_1 - P_2}{P_1 + P_2}$$

where Q refers to the quantity demanded and P to the price, and where the subscript 1 refers to the first point on a demand curve and the subscript 2 to a second point. For example, in Figure 1–2 when price falls from 60 cents to 30 cents, the elasticity is -1.91.

$$\text{elasticity} = \frac{40 - 180}{40 + 180} \bigg/ \frac{0.60 - 0.30}{0.60 + 0.30}$$

$$= \frac{-140}{220} \bigg/ \frac{0.30}{0.90}$$

$$= \frac{-21}{11}$$

While the elasticity of demand is negative, because the demand curve is negatively sloped, elasticity is discussed as if it were a positive quantity: -1.91 is said to be more elastic than -1.00.

Table 1-3   Labor Supply

WAGE (dollars per hour)	QUANTITY OF LABOR SUPPLIED (hours per year)
1.00	1,500
2.00	2,000
3.00	2,400
4.00	2,700
5.00	2,900
6.00	3,000

consumer is better off. He can buy more goods with the same money income because his real income has increased; in effect, he has more income. With a greater effective income he will buy more of ordinary goods but less of inferior goods. This produces an *income effect*: A fall in the price of a good has the effect of increasing the money income of a consumer, so that he will tend to buy a larger quantity of ordinary goods and a smaller quantity of inferior goods. Since the substitution effect increases the quantity demanded of any good as its price falls and the income effect increases the quantity demanded still further for ordinary goods, most goods follow the law of demand.[3]

In the case of labor supply, the household is a seller, not a buyer. In deciding how much labor to supply at various wage rates, the household is deciding how it shall divide its time between work and leisure. Less leisure, more work usually means more money income; and more money income means more of the things that money can buy. The choice is, then, between more consumer goods and more leisure, the demand for both of which is likely to increase as money income increases. Therefore, an increase in the wage rate may either increase or decrease the quantity of labor supplied.

Table 1–3 and Figure 1–3 present a supply curve for

---

[3] A minor exception to the law of demand is the *Giffen good*, named after the British economist Sir R. Giffen. A Giffen good is an inferior good for which the income effect is larger than the substitution effect. Bread, Giffen's example, might be such a good for the poor if it were a large item in their budgets. With a fall in the price of bread, the substitution effect would tend to increase the quantity demanded; but, if bread were an inferior good, a fall in its price, which effectively increased the income of the poor, would tend to reduce the quantity demanded. If the income effect reduced the quantity demanded by more than the substitution effect increased it, bread would be a Giffen good. The quantity demanded would fall when the price fell, which is contrary to the law of demand. Giffen goods, to be sure, are rare.

a laborer that follows the *law of supply: The higher the price, the greater the quantity supplied; the lower the price, the smaller the quantity supplied.* In this case the price is the wage rate. The law of supply, like the law of demand, assumes that other factors that influence the quantity supplied do not change. The supply curve shows how long the laborer would be willing to work at alternative wage rates, if he were free to choose the length of time he worked. If a job involves exactly a 40-hour week and a 2,000-hour year, the laborer may prefer not to work at all if the wage is too low. If he is willing to work longer than 2,000 hours a year at the going wage, he may volunteer for overtime work or seek additional part-time employment. Overtime rates of pay are typically above regular rates in order to increase the number of hours that laborers are willing to work.

The labor supply curve in Figure 1–3 is positively sloped, indicating that the quantity supplied increases as the wage rate increases. At $1.00 per hour, the laborer is willing to work 1,500 hours per year. If the hourly wage increases to $2.00, the laborer is willing to sell 2,000 hours of his labor time. As the wage rate rises above $2.00, he is willing to work even longer hours. The higher the wage rate, the greater is the quantity of labor supplied.

A labor supply curve could bend backwards, though it does not in Figure 1–3. A backward-bending supply curve can be explained in terms of the income and substitution effects. When wages rise from an initial low level, the consumer usually

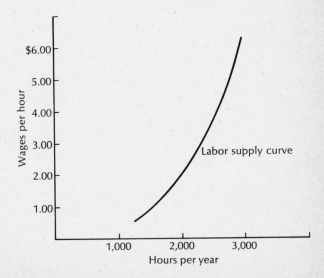

Figure 1-3   The Labor Supply Curve

prefers to substitute money income for leisure. In other words, the substitution effect is dominant, and the supply curve slopes upward to the right. Eventually, as the wage rate rises, the consumer may prefer more leisure and want to work shorter hours. The substitution effect, which induces him to substitute money income for leisure, is smaller than the income effect, which induces him to choose more leisure. This assumes that the quantity of leisure desired increases as money income increases. Whether a labor supply curve is backward bending or follows the law of supply depends on the preferences of the particular household.

The Production Function

The production function of a business enterprise describes the technical relations of inputs and outputs. *Inputs* are those factor services and products that an enterprise buys to produce the *output*, or product, that it sells. The production function for a flour mill describes what quantity and what type of wheat, labor, and machinery are needed to produce flour. The output of the flour mill in turn becomes an input for the bakery; yet, ultimately, all goods and services are produced by the factors of production—land, labor, and capital.

The production function is an essential part of economic analysis because a productive enterprise demands inputs, supplies output, and earns a profit equal to the difference between the cost of inputs and the revenue from the sale of its output. An enterprise that uses the principle of opportunity cost to calculate what quantity of inputs to buy and what quantity of output to produce must know its production function; that is, it must know how much output can be produced with various quantities and combinations of inputs.

The production function of an enterprise is often complex. Different types of inputs can be used in varying proportions to produce a given output—machines can be substituted for men, for example; the same set of inputs can be used to produce different types of goods in varying combinations—a factory can produce cars and trucks in various combinations; and output can be increased by employing more of one, some, or all the different types of inputs used in production. For the sake of simplicity, this section will focus on a single situation, in which the enterprise is assumed to produce a single good with two different inputs—labor and capital. The quantity of capital employed is assumed to be constant, because factories and equipment can not be changed over a short period of time; and the quantity of

Table 1-4   The Law of Diminishing Returns

VARIABLE INPUT[1] L	TOTAL PRODUCT[2] Q	AVERAGE PRODUCT[3] AP	MARGINAL PRODUCT[4] MP
0	0	—	
			10
1	10	10	
			8
2	18	9	
			6
3	24	8	
			4
4	28	7	
			2
5	30	6	

[1] Labor in man-years.
[2] Output in motor scooters per year.
[3] $AP = Q \div L$.
[4] $MP =$ change in $Q \div$ change in L.

labor is assumed to be variable, so that changes in output are due solely to changes in the quantity of labor. Accordingly, capital is called the *fixed* input, labor the *variable* input. In this situation the *law of diminishing returns* explains the relation between inputs and output.

The law of diminishing returns states: *As the quantity of a variable input increases, given a constant quantity of all other inputs, output eventually increases at a diminishing rate.*

Table 1–4 presents an example of the law of diminishing returns operating in a small motor scooter factory. First, consider the two columns on the left, labor input (L) and motor scooter output (Q). One man working by himself in this small plant can produce 10 motor scooters a year. If a second man comes to work, output increases to 18 motor scooters a year. Since the first man produced 10 motor scooters and the second man increased output by 8 motor scooters, output increased at a diminishing rate. As the third, fourth, and fifth men are added to the labor force, total product continues to increase, but by smaller and smaller amounts.

The third column shows the *average product* of labor (AP), which equals total product (Q) divided by labor (L). The decline in the average product of labor shows that diminishing returns occur; motor scooter output increases proportionately less than labor input.

Marginal product (MP), the fourth column, requires special consideration.[4] Marginal product is the change in total

---

[4] A mathematician would call the marginal product of labor the first derivative of output with respect to labor.

product (Q) divided by the change in the quantity of labor (L) employed. When a second man is employed, output changes from 10 to 18 motor scooters a year. The marginal product of the second man is 8 motor scooters a year. The third man adds 6 units of output, so his marginal product is only 6 motor scooters a year. The marginal product of labor declines as explained by the law of diminishing returns. The marginal product data appear in the half units in Table 1–4 because the change in output applies to the interval between one level of employment and another.

Total product, average product, and marginal product are graphed in Figure 1–4. The quantity of motor scooters produced per year appears on the vertical axis, and the quantity of labor appears on the horizontal axis. As the quantity of labor employed increases, total product increases at a diminishing rate, so that average and marginal product decline. Marginal product lies below average product because each extra laborer adds less than the average to output. A similar relation between the margin and the average exists when a baseball player bats below his average on a particular day; his marginal performance is below his average, so his average falls. Marginal product is measured vertically up from the half units of labor for the reason given before, the marginal change applies to the interval between two levels of employment.

The assumptions on which the law of diminishing returns is based need to be stressed. First, one input, in this case

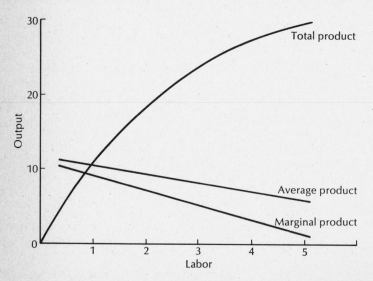

Figure 1-4   The Law of Diminishing Returns

the factory, must remain unchanged, so that an increasing quantity of the variable input (labor) is working with a constant quantity of the fixed input (capital). Second, the method of production or technology must remain unchanged. Four men working in an automated plant could easily produce more than five men working with hand tools. Technological change is important, but it is a separate issue in its own right. Third, those inputs that are employed must be used in the most efficient manner that the given technology permits. Four well-supervised workers could also produce more than five workers who were poorly supervised. The total product curve really describes the maximum feasible output from each combination of inputs. Finally, it is possible that diminishing returns might not set in at first, if the employment of a greater quantity of men permitted a greater division of labor and specialization of function. This possibility is ignored in the example of the motor scooter factory. Eventually diminishing returns must set in, for otherwise it would be possible to produce all the motor scooters in the world from a single small factory. The fixed productive capacity of a plant ultimately limits its output.

The demand for labor and the supply of output are both based on the principle of opportunity cost and the law of diminishing returns. Indeed, the demand for labor and the supply of output are directly related to each other, for once an enterprise has chosen the most profitable quantity of labor to employ, it has at the same time decided how much output to supply.

Profit is the excess of revenue over cost. In order to calculate the profit earned by our motor scooter manufacturer, it is necessary to know the price at which it sells its output and the price it pays for its inputs as well as the quantity of inputs required to produce a given volume of motor scooters. This is illustrated in Table 1–5, the first two columns of which are the same as the first two columns of Table 1–4.

Total revenue (*TR*), the third column, is calculated on the assumption that the enterprise can sell all the motor scooters it produces at $400 each. Total revenue rises from zero, where output is zero, to $4,000, where output is 10 motor scooters, to $12,000 where output is 30 motor scooters; however, it rises at a diminishing rate because output is subject to diminishing returns.

Total cost is divided into two parts: *total variable cost*, which is the cost of the variable input (labor), and *total fixed cost*, which is the cost of the fixed input (capital). Total variable cost (*TVC*), the fourth column, assumes that labor can be hired at $2,400 per man-year. This cost rises $2,400 for each additional man employed. Total fixed cost (*TFC*), the fifth column, is $1,000

Table 1-5 Diminishing Returns, Labor Demand, and Output Supply

VARIABLE INPUT[1] L (units per year)	TOTAL PRODUCT[2] Q (units per year)	TOTAL REVENUE[3] TR	TOTAL VARIABLE COST[4] TVC	TOTAL FIXED COST[5] TFC	TOTAL COST[6] TC (dollars per year)	PROFIT[7] Π	VALUE OF MARGINAL PRODUCT[8] VMP	MARGINAL COST[9] MC
0	0	0	0	1,000	1,000	(1,000)		
1	10	4,000	2,400	1,000	3,400	600	4,000	240
2	18	7,200	4,800	1,000	5,800	1,400	3,200	300
3	24	9,600	7,200	1,000	8,200	1,400	2,400	400
4	28	11,200	9,600	1,000	10,600	600	1,600	600
5	30	12,000	12,000	1,000	13,000	(1,000)	800	1,200

[1] Labor in man-years.
[2] Output in motor scooters per year.
[3] $TR = Q \times P$, where the price of motor scooters (P) is $400 each.
[4] $TVC = L \times W$, where the wage rate (W) is $2,400 per year.
[5] $TFC = \$1,000$.
[6] $TC = TVC + TFC$.
[7] $\Pi = TR - TC$.
[8] VMP = change in $TR \div$ change in $L = P \times MP$.
[9] MC = change in $TC \div$ change in $Q = W \div MP$.

a year no matter what the level of output, because the fixed input (the factory) is assumed to remain unchanged. If more capital were employed, the relation between labor and output would change, so that a whole new table of cost and revenue would have to be calculated. Total cost (*TC*) in the sixth column is simply the sum of total variable and total fixed cost.

Profit (II), the seventh column, equals total revenue minus total cost. Profit rises from a negative $1,000 (that is, a loss of $1,000) where output is zero to a maximum of $1,400 where 18 or 24 motor scooters are produced, and then falls again. If the production function on which these profit calculations are based were continuous, instead of varying in discrete steps one man-year at a time, profit would be at a maximum between the points of 18 and 24 units of output or, what amounts to the same thing, approximately at the point where two and one-half laborers are employed.[5]

The profits of the motor scooter factory are maximized by applying the principle of opportunity cost and choosing that input-output alternative which offers the greatest profit. In Table 1–5 the profit-maximizing manager would choose either to demand two man-years of labor and to supply 18 units of output or to demand three man-years of labor and to supply 24 motor scooters, since both alternatives yield the same profit. If either the wage of labor or the price of the motor scooter were to change, the point of maximum profit would tend to change and so would the quantity of labor demanded and the number of motor scooters supplied.

The demand schedule for labor shows how much labor is demanded at various wage rates and can be calculated from the data presented in Table 1–5. In deciding how much labor to employ, the factory manager needs to know how much extra revenue an extra laborer will produce. If the marginal laborer adds more to revenue than to cost, profits will be increased by employing him. If, however, the last laborer adds less to revenue than to cost, profits will be increased by reducing the work force. Thus, the demand for labor is explained by the extra revenue generated by the marginal laborer. In Table 1–5 the first laborer adds $4,000 to total revenue, the second adds $3,200, the third adds $2,400, and so on. The extra revenue that each extra laborer produces declines, not because the best workers are hired first, but because the marginal product of labor declines

---

[5] A continuous schedule of profits would reach an approximate maximum of $1,500 at 2½ laborers and 21¼ units of output.

because of the law of diminishing returns. This is true even though all the laborers are equally capable.

The demand schedule for labor can be calculated in a simple manner when the price of the product is constant, as it is in Table 1–5. The *value of the marginal product* of labor (*VMP*), which appears in the eighth column, is the demand schedule for labor because it shows for how much the extra output produced by each additional laborer sells. The value of the marginal product equals the marginal product (*MP*) multiplied by the price (*P*) of the product. The value of the marginal product of the first laborer is $4,000, 10 motor scooters at $400 each; the second laborer has a value of the marginal product of $3,200, 8 motor scooters at $400 each, and so on. If the wage rate (*W*) is $3,200 or less, it is profitable to hire the second laborer. Profits are maximized where the value of the marginal product equals the wage (*VMP=W*), that is, where the extra revenue equals the extra cost. As long as the extra revenue (*VMP*) exceeds the extra cost (*W*), profits can be increased by hiring more labor.

The demand curve for labor (*VMP*) is graphed in Figure 1–5. It declines to the right and follows the law of demand —the lower the wage, the greater the quantity demanded. The value of the marginal product is measured vertically up from the half unit of labor, because the margin applies to the distance between one unit and another. At a wage of $2,400 per man-year, two and one-half laborers are employed. If fewer laborers were employed, the extra revenue (*VMP*) would exceed the extra cost (*W*); profits could be increased by employing more labor. If more than two and one-half laborers were employed, the extra cost (*W*) would exceed the extra revenue (*VMP*), and reducing the work force would increase profits. Profits are maximized where *VMP=W*.

The supply schedule for output shows how much will be supplied at various prices. Here the business manager needs to know whether an extra unit of output adds more to revenue than to cost; if it does, profits can be increased by increasing output. When the extra revenue exactly equals the extra cost, profits can not be increased by changing the volume of output, and the quantity of output to be supplied is determined.

In Table 1–5 each extra laborer increases output by smaller and smaller amounts, but each extra laborer costs $2,400 per man-year; therefore, the cost of each extra unit of output rises. It rises because of the law of diminishing returns. The change in total cost divided by the change in output is called *marginal cost* (*MC*), the last column in Table 1–5. When the firm can sell all its output at the market price, that is, when it is a price-taker and not a price-setter, the marginal cost curve is the

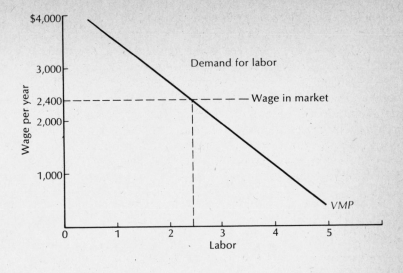

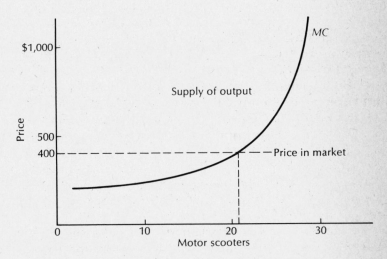

Figure 1-5   Demand for Labor and Supply of Output

supply curve for the firm. In this situation, the market price equals the extra revenue that the firm derives from selling an extra unit of output. Profits are maximized when price equals marginal cost ($P = MC$).

The marginal cost data in Table 1–5 are graphed in Figure 1–5, in which marginal cost is measured vertically up from the mid-points between successive levels of output. When output increases from 10 to 18 motor scooters a year, the marginal cost is $300 per unit. Strictly speaking, this $300 a unit does not apply to either the tenth or the eighteenth motor scooter but to some unit between. When output increases from 18 to 24 units a year, marginal cost is $400. One additional laborer, whose marginal product is 6 scooters, is employed for $2,400. Marginal cost is, then, $2,400 divided by 6 motor scooters, or $400 a scooter. This is a quick way to calculate marginal cost $(MC = W \div MP)$. If the market price were $600, however, the marginal cost would be less than the price at which additional output could be sold. Profits could be increased by increasing output, that is, by supplying a greater quantity of output (say 26 units). Thus, the marginal cost curve is the supply curve for the firm. It follows the law of supply—the higher the price, the greater the quantity supplied.[6]

Equilibrium

Prices are determined by the activities of buyers and sellers in the market. As a matter of self-interest, buyers try to purchase goods and services at as low a price as possible, and sellers try to earn as large an income as possible. Buyers cannot be forced to buy if the price is too high, and sellers cannot be forced to sell if the price is too low. Both are free to act in their own self-interest, and neither will act unless he gains from an exchange, though one may gain more than another. The higgling and bargaining of the market tend to establish a price at which buyers and sellers agree to exchange one thing for another.

Equilibrium exists in a market at that price where the quantity demanded equals the quantity supplied. In the consumer goods market, the quantity demanded at each price equals how much all consumers together are willing to buy at each price, while the quantity supplied shows how much all producers together are willing to sell at each price. Similarly, in the labor and other factor markets, demand is the sum of the quantities demanded by productive enterprises and supply is the sum of the quantities supplied at each price (or wage) level. Market demand curves generally follow the law of demand—the lower the price, the greater the quantity demanded; and in most cases market supply curves follow the law of supply—the higher the price, the greater the quantity supplied. The supply and demand curves for cups of coffee in Table 1–6 and Figure 1–6 illustrate the principle of equilibrium.

---

[6] One qualification should be noted. The firm would be better off to shut down if total revenue did not cover total variable cost. The most it needs to lose is its fixed cost.

Table 1-6   Supply and Demand for Coffee

PRICE PER CUP (cents)	QUANTITY DEMANDED (millions of cups a year)	QUANTITY SUPPLIED (millions of cups a year)
25	200	550
20	300	500
15	400	400
10	500	250
5	600	50

To be precise, the supply and demand analysis in Figure 1–6 only explains the equilibrium price and quantity in a *competitive* market. Competitive markets are defined in terms of three conditions: (1) there are many buyers and sellers, each of whom is so small relative to the size of the market that no one of them can influence the equilibrium price; (2) the product is homogeneous, that is, the subjective preferences of consumers are such that the output of one seller is considered to be the same as the output of other sellers, and (3) entry is free into the market, that is, all sellers have equal access to inputs, technology, and so on. Competitive markets adjust to the equilibrium point quickly when buyers and sellers have perfect knowledge of the market and are perfectly mobile to act on their knowledge. Some commodity markets come close to meeting these conditions (for example, the market for frozen pork bellies on the Chicago

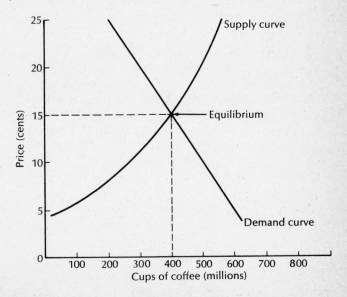

Figure 1-6   Supply and Demand for Coffee

Mercantile Exchange), but such markets are an exception rather than the rule. Most markets are influenced by a degree of monopoly power (that is, sellers are relatively few, products are differentiated, or entry is restricted), which means that individual producers have some control over prices. Monopolists need not take the price in the market as given, but can restrict supply and set price above marginal cost. The theory of supply and demand in competitive markets is a simplification and only a first step to understanding the determination of market prices.

In Figure 1–6 the demand curve shows the quantity of coffee that consumers as a group would buy at various prices. If the price were 25 cents a cup, consumers would demand 200 million cups a year; at 20 cents they would demand a larger quantity, 300 million cups. In the same way, the supply curve shows how much coffee restaurants would be willing to sell at various prices. The market supply curve is the sum of the marginal cost curves of individual sellers and is based on the assumption that the productive capacity (capital) available for making coffee is fixed for the period of time under consideration. At 10 cents a cup they would be willing to supply 250 million cups and at 15 cents they would be willing to increase their supply to 400 million cups. The market is in equilibrium where the quantity supplied equals the quantity demanded, that is, at 15 cents a cup. At 15 cents a cup consumers demand and restaurants supply 400 million cups.

The process by which the market reaches an equilibrium point varies from market to market. In a competitive market, however, no individual has the power to set the price, though each individual can alter the price he bids or asks. On the one hand, when the price is above the equilibrium level, an excess supply exists. The quantity supplied exceeds the quantity demanded. For example, in Figure 1–6 at 20 cents a cup consumers demand only 300 million cups, while restaurants are willing to sell 500 million cups. Some sellers can not find buyers at so high a price; and, since they are willing to sell for less, they lower their prices. As the price falls, the quantity demanded rises and the quantity supplied falls until equilibrium is established. On the other hand, below the equilibrium price an excess demand exists. The quantity demanded exceeds the quantity supplied. At 10 cents a cup, for example, consumers demand 500 million cups, but restaurants supply only 250 million cups a year. Some consumers would rather pay more than go without, so they bid up the price until equilibrium is reached. In equilibrium the quantity supplied equals the quantity demanded.

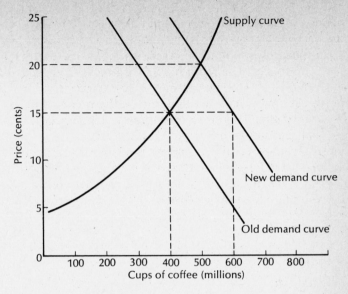

Figure 1-7   A Shift in Demand

From time to time demand and supply curves shift. These curves shift when transactors change the quantities they are willing to buy or sell at given prices. The demand curve for coffee might shift out, for example, if consumer income increased or if the price of tea rose. This is illustrated in Figure 1–7, where consumers increase their demand by 200 million cups a year at each price level. The supply curve could also shift if, for example, restaurants were to pay lower wages, use more capital, or employ more efficient equipment. This possibility is left to the reader to study.[7]

In Figure 1–7 the supply curve is the same as before, but the new demand curve is farther out from the origin than the old demand curve. At the old equilibrium price (15 cents), 600 million cups of coffee are now demanded but only 400 million are supplied. There is an excess demand. Consumers, therefore, bid up the price. As the price rises, the quantity demanded falls and the quantity supplied rises until a new equilibrium is established at 20 cents a cup, at which price both demand and supply are 500 million cups a year.

The shift in the demand curve in Figure 1–7 increased

---

[7] Hint: At a lower wage rate the marginal cost curve of each producer would fall ($MC = W \div MP$). More capital or more efficient equipment would increase the output per worker and thus reduce variable costs.

the quantity supplied, but the supply curve did not shift. There was a movement along the existing supply curve as buyers bid up prices. The quantity supplied increased as the price rose.

Supply and demand help allocate resources in a competitive economy. An upward shift in the demand for coffee, which increases the price of coffee, makes the production of coffee more profitable. Therefore, restaurants will supply a greater quantity than before. If the coffee crop fails in Brazil, a shortage will occur and the price will tend to rise. The supply curve will shift up and to the left, because each cup of coffee will cost more to produce. As the price rises, some consumers will buy a smaller quantity and others may buy none at all. Thus, the reduced supply is allocated to those consumers who are willing to pay the most.

PRIVATE AND SOCIAL ACCOUNTING

Private and social accounting are large and complicated subjects that would require books to survey. This chapter is concerned only with those aspects of accounting that are essential to macroeconomic theory. Private accounting refers to the record keeping of individual transactors, especially business enterprises. Households could keep systematic records but few do. Social accounting keeps track of transactions made by groups of transactors, such as all producers. The principal social accounts treated in this chapter are the national income accounts, the financial flow accounts, and the balance-of-payments account. These accounts, which are mainly derived from private records, are kept and published by the federal government.

Private Accounting

Private accounts record the transactions of business enterprises so that businessmen know how well they are doing. Transactions are recorded by a system of double entry bookkeeping. A balance sheet summarizes what is owned and owed, and an income statement shows whether a business earned a profit. A discussion of each of these topics is followed by a brief explanation of the relation between the balance sheet and the income statement.

Double Entry Bookkeeping   Double entry bookkeeping arose during the Middle Ages as commerce revived in western Europe after the fall of Rome. Records were kept by a system of double entries because of the nature of a transaction. If a merchant from Lucca carried a yard of silk to the fair at Troyes and sold it to a merchant from London for 72 English pennies, he would make two entries in his books: (1) the value of the silk he sold and (2) the amount of money he received, both with the same date. The merchant from London would do the same in reverse.

Each transaction takes place at a point in time and involves at least two parties, a buyer and a seller. Each party gives one thing for another: silk is exchanged for money at the same time money is exchanged for silk. In exchange the silk and the money are of equal value, but the value of the silk is expressed in terms of money. Since it is the nature of a transaction that each party gives up one item and receives another item of equal value, each party makes a double entry in his books.

A transaction equates one value with another and can be expressed by an equation of exchange. In the case of the silk transaction the equation is

1 yard silk = 72 pennies

The value of the silk is expressed in terms of pennies, but the value of a penny can also be expressed in terms of silk. One could say, "An English penny is worth one-half inch of silk," which would sound odd to an Englishman but would be clear to a silk merchant not familiar with pennies.

When one currency is exchanged for another, the transaction is often expressed both ways. Suppose the silk merchant from Lucca took his 72 English pennies to a money changer to obtain gold florins. If the transaction is

72 pennies = 2 florins

the price can be expressed in terms of either currency: the price of a florin is 36 pennies, the price of a penny is 1/36th of a florin. The price of anything is its value in exchange. It states the ratio at which two quantities are exchanged.

The merchant from Lucca must decide which currency to use in bookkeeping; that is, he must choose a unit of account. In order to add up his sales, all sales must be expressed in the same terms. If he used florins instead of pennies, he would record the sale of one yard of silk as if it had been in exchange for florins, even though he actually received English pennies.

Accountants use the terms "debit" and "credit" for the two parts of a transaction, which are abbreviated Dr. and Cr., respectively. If the Lucca merchant recorded his transactions in a general journal, he would enter the silk transaction as shown in Table 2–1. He debits the cash he receives and credits the sale of

Table 2-1   General Journal (florins)

DATE	DESCRIPTION	DR.	CR.
1273 May 1	Cash Sales Sale of 1 yd. silk to an Englishman	2	2

silk. The terms debit and credit should not be confused with the terms debtor and creditor. The debits appear on the left and credits on the right by convention.

The Balance Sheet   The *balance sheet* shows, at a point in time, how much a business enterprise owns in total, how much it owes to others, and how much it is worth in net, that is, after deducting what is owed to others. It is prepared as of the end of an accounting period, say as of midnight December 31, so that the record at the end of one period is the same as that at the beginning of the next period. Many companies prepare balance sheets quarterly and even monthly as well as annually. What an enterprise owns are called its *assets*, what it owes are its *liabilities*, and its *net worth* is its assets minus its liabilities.

Assets appear on the left side of Table 2–2. Conventional accounting statements classify assets as current assets or fixed assets. Current assets include cash in the form of currency and bank deposits, accounts receivable from customers who buy on credit, inventories of goods and materials, and other items that can be converted into cash within a short period of time.

Table 2-2   Balance Sheet

SUPER PENCIL CORPORATION DECEMBER 31, 1973 (thousands of dollars)				
ASSETS			**LIABILITIES**	
Financial assets:			Current liabilities:	
Cash	100		Accounts payable	50
Accounts receivable	250		Bank loan	100
Total financial assets		350	Total current liabilities	150
			Long-term liabilities:	
Nonfinancial assets:			Bond (7% due 1990)	500
Inventory	200		Total liabilities	650
Equipment	300		Net worth:	
Building	800		Paid-in capital	1,000
Land	400		Retained earnings	400
Total nonfinancial assets		1,700	Total net worth	1,400
Total assets		2,050	*Total claims on assets*	2,050

say a year. Fixed assets are durable and ordinarily last more than one year; examples are equipment, buildings, and land. In Table 2–2 assets are classified as financial or nonfinancial in order to relate the balance sheet to the social accounts. Financial assets are claims against other parties, such as accounts receivable. Cash is also a claim against other parties, because it is accepted by them; it is a generalized claim that everyone recognizes in settlement of obligations. Nonfinancial assets are tangible property like inventory, equipment, buildings, and land.

Liabilities show how much a company owes to others. They are IOUs and appear on the right side of Table 2–2. Liabilities due within a year are classified as current liabilities; those with a greater maturity are classified as long-term liabilities. The net worth of a company, which equals total assets minus total liabilities, represents the owners' claim on a company. The paid-in capital is the amount of funds that the owners have invested in the company. Retained earnings are profits that have not been paid out, but credited to the account of the owners. When a company is dissolved and its assets sold, the proceeds are used first to pay off all IOUs. Whatever is left belongs to the owners. Thus, both liabilities and net worth are claims on the assets of a company. Both are financial items.

The balance sheets of many companies contain more categories than those presented in Table 2–2. For example, the paid-in capital of a corporation may include both common stock and preferred stock. Preferred stockholders are ordinarily entitled to a share in the profits of a company before common stock-holders. The names used to identify items may also differ. A proprietorship may refer to the net worth account as proprietor's equity. However, all balance sheets are based on the same equation:

$$\text{total assets} = \text{total liabilities} + \text{net worth}$$

If the total assets increased from the end of one period to another, the claims on those assets must increase because of the nature of double entry accounting.

The Income Statement   The *income statement* reports the profit or loss that a business earns over a period of time, such as a year. It is often called a *profit and loss statement*. Like the balance sheet, the income statement is prepared quarterly and some-times monthly as well as annually; but, unlike the balance sheet, it summarizes only the operations of an enterprise that relate to the profits attributable to a particular period. During the accounting period an enterprise sells goods and services in exchange for funds. It allocates these funds first to those expenses that are attributable to the operations of the period and then to profit. Thus, the basic equation of the income statement is

$$\text{revenue} = \text{expenses} + \text{profit}$$

When expenses exceed revenue, the difference is a loss.

The measurement of profit involves a number of difficulties. The profit earned in one period needs to be distinguished from the profit earned in another period, and the profit earned from ordinary operations needs to be distinguished from extraordinary events. To calculate profit, revenue and expense should reflect the ordinary operations of a business during a given period. This makes it possible to compare one period with another and determine whether business is improving. The income statement in Table 2-3 reports revenue and expenses from operations for one year.

Sales are the only revenue in Table 2-3, but revenue could also include interest, dividends, and rent from investments and properties. For a bank the principal revenue would be interest. All the income from a business' ordinary operations is entered as revenue. However, if a manufacturer sold one of its factories, the sale would not be reported as revenue but as an extraordinary gain or loss, because manufacturing is its ordinary business. An insurance payment for a factory that burned down would also be an extraordinary source of funds.

Expenditures are often made in one period, but allocated to another period. This is especially true of inventory and

Table 2-3   Income Statement

SUPER PENCIL CORPORATION, JANUARY 1, 1973, TO DECEMBER 31, 1973
(thousands of dollars)

Revenue:			
Sales			1,700
Expenses:			
Purchases		800	
Change in inventory:			
Opening inventory	200		
less: Closing inventory	240		
Change in inventory		− 40	
Wages and salaries		500	
Depreciation		110	
Interest paid		45	
Total expenses			1,415
Corporate profits before tax:			
Corporate profits tax	140		
Dividends	100		
Undistributed profit	45		
Corporate profits before tax			285

fixed assets. Table 2–3 reports the purchases of goods and services by the enterprise during the year and subtracts the change
in the inventory of goods on hand. Since the inventory at the end
of the year exceeded the inventory at the start of the year, the
value of inventory increased during the year. The cost of that
increase in inventory should not be deducted from sales in calculating profits for the current year, because that inventory can
be sold only in the future. If inventories were to decline, the
cost of the inventory used up would be attributable to current
sales, and that cost should be counted as a current operating
expense.[1] Plant and equipment are fixed assets that are used up
over the course of their lives. The amount by which they are
used up during the current year is a current operating expense,
which should be deducted from revenue in calculating profit.
The current cost of plant and equipment used up or consumed is
called *depreciation,* or *capital consumption.*[2] The other expenses
in Table 2–3 are self-explanatory.

---

[1] The valuation of inventory is particularly complicated when the price of
goods purchased changes or when raw materials are turned into finished
inventory by a manufacturer.
[2] Depreciation costs cannot be known for certain and must be estimated. The
so-called straight-line method is widely used: the original cost minus the
expected scrap value is divided equally over the expected life of the asset.

Revenue minus expense equals profit—in this case, corporate profits before tax. The tax on corporate profits is the amount attributable to current operations, regardless of when it is paid. When the tax is paid with a delay, it is said to be *accrued* or a *tax liability*. Dividends are paid to the owners, while undistributed profits are retained within the corporation and increase the net worth on its balance sheet.

The Relation Between the Balance Sheet and the Income Statement   The relation between the balance sheet and the income statement is important to business finance and to macroeconomic theory. Since this book is more concerned with economics than with business, this relation is stated using terms that are more common in social accounting than in private accounting. The point of view of the social accounts differs from that of business accounts. In business accounts, sales are treated as values given up, in exchange for which funds are received; and expenses are treated as values received, in exchange for which funds are paid. In the social accounts, sales are measured by the inflow of funds, expenses by the outflow of funds. An inflow is called a *source* of funds and an outflow a *use* of funds. In terms of the circular flow diagram, private accounting focuses on goods and services, whereas social accounting summarizes transactions in terms of the flow of funds.

The balance sheet measures a stock, an accumulation of value at a point in time; the income statement measures a flow, an amount of value exchanged over a period of time. A physical analogy is a lake with a river flowing in and a river flowing out. The lake is a given volume at any point in time; it is a stock. Rivers are flows, which are measured in gallons per minute or day. The flows and the stock are related; if more flows in than flows out, the stock increases. Stocks and flows are used throughout economic analysis.

A balance sheet at the beginning of a year, the income statement for the year, and a balance sheet at the end of the year appear in Table 2–4. The first balance sheet is dated as of the end of 1972, which is the same as the beginning of 1973. It is like the balance sheet in Table 2–2 except for a few items. The income statement is the same as Table 2–3, though the subtotals have been omitted. Three items in the income statement, which are marked with an asterisk (*), must affect the closing balance sheet: inventories, depreciation, and undistributed profits. Inventories accumulated during the year, so the closing balance sheet records a greater value than the opening balance sheet. The equipment and the original building, which is referred to as building A,

Table 2-4   Balance Sheets and Income Statement (thousands of dollars)

BALANCE SHEET I   DECEMBER 31, 1972

Financial assets:		Liabilities:	
Cash	100	Bank loan	100
		Bond	500
Nonfinancial assets:			
Inventory	200	Net worth:	
Equipment	300	Paid–in capital	1,000
Building A	800	Retained earnings	200
Land	400		
Total assets	1,800	*Total claims on assets*	1,800

INCOME STATEMENT   JANUARY 1, 1973, TO DECEMBER 31, 1973

Purchases	800	Sales	1,700
Change in inventory	− 40*		
Wages and salaries	500		
Depreciation	110*		
Interest	45		
Corporate profits tax	140		
Dividends	100		
Undistributed profit	45*		
Allocations	1,700	*Proceeds*	1,700

BALANCE SHEET II   DECEMBER 31, 1973

Financial assets:		Liabilities:	
Cash	60*	Bank loan	55*
		Bonds	590*
Nonfinancial assets:			
Inventory	240*	Net worth:	
Equipment	270*	Paid–in capital	1,000
Building A	720*	Retained earnings	245*
Building B	200*		
Land	400		
Total assets	1,890	*Total claims on assets*	1,890

depreciated during the year at the rate of 10 percent each. A total of $110,000 worth of equipment and building were used up in production, the value of which was transferred to the goods sold and counted as a current expense. Finally, undistributed profits increased the net worth of the corporation by $45,000. The closing balance sheet reports these changes plus a number of financial and capital transactions that were unrelated to the calculation of current earnings and, therefore, were not reported in the income statement.

All the items that changed from the opening to the closing balance sheet are marked with an asterisk. In addition to the three already mentioned, cash and bank loans declined, a new building was purchased, and additional bonds issued. From the point of view of economic analysis, these changes are more easily understood when they are organized in a different manner, which is the purpose of Tables 2–5 and 2–6.

Table 2–5 is a *capital account*, which distinguishes between the financial and nonfinancial items in the balance sheet. A financial item is an IOU or claim; a nonfinancial item is tangible property. Nonfinancial items are given special consideration because they form two of the principal factors of production—capital and land. From the point of view of an individual firm, capital acquisitions are the quantity of newly acquired nonfinancial assets. In this case, the corporation invested $40,000 in inventory and $200,000 in a new building, denoted B. From the point of view of the economy as a whole, capital acquisitions include only newly produced goods; transactions in existing assets (such as land) cancel out because they increase the assets of the buyer by the same amount that they decrease the assets of the seller.

Table 2-5   Capital Account, 1973 (thousands of dollars)

USES		SOURCES		
Building B	200	Inside funds.		
Change in inventory	+ 40	Depreciation	110	
		Undistributed profits	45	
		Inside funds		155
		Funds raised		85
Capital acquisitions	240	*Sources of funds*		240

New capital acquisitions appear on the left side of Table 2–5 as a use of funds. The sources of funds that finance this investment appear on the right side. The corporation had $110,000 in depreciation costs that were not paid out but remained inside the corporation. It also had $45,000 in profits that were not distributed to the owners in the form of dividends. Depreciation plus undistributed profits are called the *inside* funds of the corporation. Since capital acquisitions exceeded inside funds, the corporation had to raise funds through financial channels; that is, it ran a deficit on its capital account. Funds raised were $85,000.

Table 2–6 reports how the corporation raised funds to finance its capital acquisitions. Funds can be raised in two ways: by an increase in liabilities or by a decrease in financial

Table 2-6   Funds Raised, 1973 (thousands of dollars)

USES		SOURCES	
Funds raised	85	Change in liabilities:	
		Bank loan	−45
		Bond	90
		less: Change in financial assets:	
		Cash	40
Funds raised	85	*Financial sources of funds*	85

assets. In this case both were used, as can be seen by comparing the opening and closing balance sheets. It issued $90,000 in bonds; but, since it reduced its bank loan by $45,000, liabilities increased only $45,000 in net. It also reduced its cash balances by $40,000 to help finance its capital acquisitions. The $45,000 increase in liabilities plus the $40,000 decrease in financial assets provided the $85,000 in funds raised ($85 = 45 + 40$).

Only the net change in financial items appears in Table 2–6. During the course of the year, its cash balances alone changed from day to day and involved a much larger volume of transactions than the total cash balance at any point in time. The other financial items on the balance sheet may change more than once. The difference between opening and closing balance sheets indicates only the net change over the year.

Before passing on to social accounting, four basic equations should be learned.

1. Balance sheet:
   assets = liabilities + net worth
2. Income statement:
   revenue = expenses + profit
3. Capital account:
   capital acquisitions = inside funds + funds raised
4. Funds raised to finance a capital deficit:
   funds raised = change in liabilities − change in financial assets

All of these equations are used in social accounting.

Social Accounting

Social accounting provides a theoretical framework for the collection and publication of economic statistics. The usual emphasis is on the statistics, such as the gross national product (GNP), which measures production. This section stresses the theoretical or conceptual framework, which shows the relation between one statistic and another and between one sector of the economy and another. A great amount of detail is omitted in presenting this framework. A separate section presents the detail of the gross national product account for the United States and a graph of the growth in GNP per capita for a number of countries over the last two decades.

Social accounting summarizes transactions that occur between aggregate groups of economic agents: producers, consumers, government, and so on. Unlike private accounting, social accounting records a transaction for both parties, for both the buyer and the seller. This requires at least four sets of entries instead of two and is called *quadruple entry* accounting. For example, when a producer sells an automobile to a consumer, the producer sector records the sale as an inflow of funds and records the allocation of those funds among expenses and profit as an outflow of funds; the consumer sector records an outflow of funds for the automobile and an inflow of funds for the factor services sold to the producer who made the automobile. Transactions within a group cancel out; the account for each group is said to be *consolidated*. In the example of the automobile transaction, the purchase of parts and materials by one manufacturer from another does not appear in the consolidated producer account, because the price of an automobile includes the value of all the goods and services that went into it; only transactions between the producer sector and other sectors appear.

Three social accounting systems are considered: the national income accounts (NIA), which trace the flow of funds between producers and the ultimate purchasers of output; the financial flow accounts, which record financial transactions between the purchasing sectors; and the balance-of-payments account, which shows both nonfinancial and financial transactions between a nation state and the rest of the world.[3] All three accounting systems are assumed to be constructed on a compatible basis, even though the actual published accounts are often incompatible and vary substantially from nation to nation.

National Income Accounts   The national income accounts measure the flows of goods and services that are depicted by the circular flow diagram. Output is sold by the producer sector to

---

[3] Two other social accounts used in economic analysis are the input-output table, which focuses on transactions between various industries within the producer sector, and the national wealth account, which is a balance sheet for a nation.

Table 2–7 Outline of the National Income Accounts, 1972 (billions of dollars)

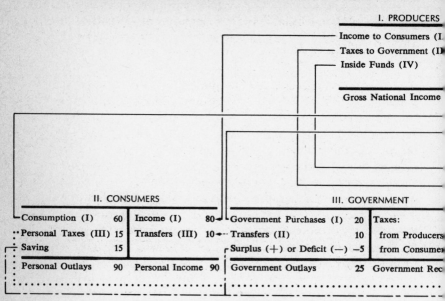

I. PRODUCERS

Income to Consumers (I

Taxes to Government (II

Inside Funds (IV)

Gross National Income

II. CONSUMERS		III. GOVERNMENT	
Consumption (I) 60	Income (I) 80	Government Purchases (I) 20	Taxes:
Personal Taxes (III) 15	Transfers (III) 10	Transfers (II) 10	from Producers
Saving 15		Surplus (+) or Deficit (−) −5	from Consumer
Personal Outlays 90	Personal Income 90	Government Outlays 25	Government Rec

four purchasing sectors: consumers, government, investors, and the rest of the world. Each purchasing sector is treated as an aggregate group. The transactions of producers appear in one account, while the transactions of the four purchasing sectors appear in four separate accounts. A simplified outline of these accounts is presented in Table 2–7.

The first account shows the sources and uses of funds for the producer sector. The sources of funds are the four components of aggregate demand: consumption, government purchases, investment, and net exports (exports minus imports). The sum of these four components equals the gross national product, which measures the total output of goods and services during the year valued at current market prices. The funds that the producer sector receives for its output are allocated among consumers, government, and investors. Consumers sell factor services to producers in exchange for wages and salaries; interest, dividends, and rent; and net income of self-employed persons, such as doctors, lawyers, and farmers. Government receives corporate profit taxes and other taxes paid by business enterprises, such as sales taxes and property taxes. Subsidies are treated as a negative tax. Inside funds are capital consumption (depreciation) plus undistributed corporate profits, which are retained by business and viewed as

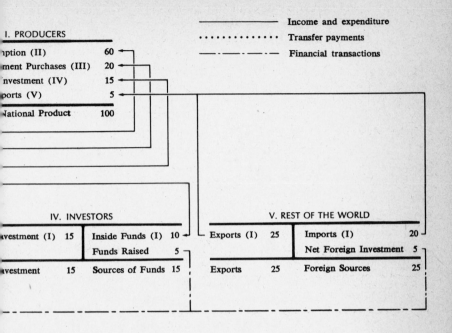

I. PRODUCERS

...ption (II)	60
...ment Purchases (III)	20
...nvestment (IV)	15
...ports (V)	5
...National Product	100

Income and expenditure
Transfer payments
Financial transactions

IV. INVESTORS

...vestment (I)	15	Inside Funds (I)	10
		Funds Raised	5
...vestment	15	Sources of Funds	15

V. REST OF THE WORLD

Exports (I)	25	Imports (I)	20
		Net Foreign Investment	5
Exports	25	Foreign Sources	25

going to the investor sector. Each of the items in the first account is followed by a roman numeral indicating the purchasing account with which the transaction is made.

The term gross national product (GNP) needs some explanation. First, "product" means that GNP measures production, or output. Second, "national" identifies the producers as nationals, or persons normally resident in a country. The United Nations accounts use the concept of gross domestic product, total production within the geographic boundaries of a country. Third, "gross" is used because investment includes all newly produced capital goods without deducting capital consumption (depreciation). Some of the new capital goods merely replace those that are used up in production. Net investment is the increase in the stock of capital goods after deducting the consumption of capital that occurs during production.

GNP can be measured by collecting statistics on the value of goods sold to the purchasing sectors. It can also be measured by the flow of income and tax payments from producers to the purchasing sectors, because gross national product equals gross national income. Every dollar spent is a dollar received. In practice, statistical estimates of the two sides of the account are not equal, the difference being a statistical discrepancy. A third way to measure GNP is to compute the value added to production by each enterprise. If an automobile manufacturer purchases materials and parts worth $1 million that are ultimately sold for $3 million, it has added $2 million in value to its purchases. That $2 million is allocated to profit and expenses, excluding purchases from other producers. The value added to output at each step in production from the mine to the factory to the consumer measures the price paid by the consumer. The sum of the value added in production by all producers equals gross national product.

The statistics that the government uses to compute GNP come from the income statements and balance sheets that business enterprises file when they pay their taxes and from the income tax returns of individuals. In addition, the government and a number of private agencies collect data on the production and sale of particular products, such as automobiles, television sets, construction contracts, and so on. In the United States, the task of fitting all these sources of information together belongs to the Bureau of Economic Analysis (formerly the Office of Business Economics).

The consumer sector includes private nonprofit organizations, such as private schools and churches, as well as households. Income is received and consumption goods are purchased from producers. When income is received in kind, the board and room of a farmhand, for example, it is treated as if the income were paid and the board and room were purchased in cash. Such transactions, of which there are a wide variety, are said to be *imputed*.[4] In addition to income received for factor services performed, consumers receive *transfer payments* from the government. A transfer payment is an expenditure that does not involve the purchase of output, factor services, or IOUs. Government transfer payments include social welfare payments and interest on the public debt. Personal taxes are a transfer from consumers to government.

The income that consumers receive from producers plus the transfer payments that they receive from government equals *personal income*. Personal income minus personal taxes equals *personal disposable income*, or what consumers have available to spend or save. *Personal saving* is the financial surplus that consumers have left after paying taxes and buying goods and services. Depositing money in the bank is perhaps the most obvi-

---

[4] Imputations are also made for persons who own and occupy their home, for food produced and consumed on the farm, and so on.

ous way to save, but consumers also save by increasing any of their financial assets or by reducing their liabilities. Many consumers increase their financial assets by contributing to a pension plan or by making life insurance payments at the same time they are making payments on consumer credit accounts and mortgages.

The government sector covers only general government activities and not government-owned business-type activities. The revenue of government-owned business-type enterprises comes primarily from the sale of services or goods rather than from taxes. Public water works, the post office, canals, toll roads, publicly-owned electric utilities, liquor stores, and city bus lines all sell goods and services to the public; therefore, they are treated as if they were private enterprises. The net income of such enterprises is a source of funds to the government, though it is omitted from Table 2–7. Subsidies are also omitted.

Most of the items in the government account have already been discussed. Taxes come from producers and from persons. Expenditures are purchases of output and transfers of funds to consumers. When receipts exceed expenditures, the government has a surplus; when expenditures exceed receipts, there is a deficit; and, when expenditures equal receipts, the government has a balanced budget. In Table 2–7 the government has a deficit of $5 billion on the national income account.[5] This deficit is ordinarily financed by issuing bonds or other IOUs,[6] that is, by increasing liabilities; but it could be financed by reducing the financial assets of the government, such as government bank deposits. The total liabilities of the government are often referred to as the national debt.

The investor account is similar to the capital account presented earlier for a single enterprise. Gross investment as measured in this account is investment in newly produced capital goods, not investment in land or used capital goods, which cancel out, and not investment in financial assets, which fall under the heading of funds raised. By convention, gross investment includes the purchase of new housing by consumers as well as the accumulation of inventories and the purchase of new structures and equipment by enterprises, including government business-type enterprises. If gross investment exceeds inside

---

[5] In the newspapers the government deficit often refers to special government accounts, of which there are several, that are not constructed on the same basis as the NIA.
[6] In times of distress governments occasionally finance their deficits by printing money, which is a sort of IOU.

funds, the deficit is financed by increasing liabilities or by reducing financial assets.

Net exports are the fourth component of aggregate demand. All the goods and services produced in a nation are purchased either by residents or by nonresidents. Purchases by nonresidents are called exports. Residents purchase goods and services produced at home and imported from abroad. Since imports are counted once in the consumer, investor, and government components of aggregate demand, they are subtracted from exports to avoid double counting. Net exports, the difference between exports and imports, measure the net purchases of national output by nonresidents.

The rest of the world account, account V in Figure 2–7, is constructed from the point of view of foreign countries, but the entries in the account refer to the exports, imports, and net foreign investment of the country for which the GNP account is constructed, hereafter referred to as the home country. The exports of the home country are a use of funds by the rest of the world, and its imports are a source of funds to the rest of the world. When its exports exceed its imports, as in Table 2–7, the home country has a surplus, while the rest of the world has a deficit. The rest of the world finances that deficit by increasing its liabilities to the home country or by reducing its holdings of financial assets that are claims on the home country. In other words, the home country holds more claims on the rest of the world, on net. This net increase in claims is called the *net foreign investment* of the home country.

The national income accounts form an interlocking network that is theoretically important.[7] In the instant that a transaction occurs, at least four and often more entries can be made. The funds that a seller receives are all allocated to one or another use, and all the funds that a buyer spends have a source. Consider the following case, in which (1) government increases its purchases of output $5 billion by running a deficit, (2) producers use all $5 billion to pay labor, and (3) consumers save all their new income. The first entry records the government purchase in the producer account. This purchase is a component of GNP and increases income, which could be allocated among income to persons, taxes to government, and inside funds to bus-

---

[7] The interlocking nature of the NIA is obscured by the fact that transactors keep their accounts on different bases. Business typically keeps accounts on an accrual basis; that is, wages, taxes, and so on are assumed to be paid before they are actually paid. Consumers think in terms of cash accounting; that is, income is not counted until the cash is received.

iness. However, in this case consumers, as wage earners, receive all the income from the increase in GNP. The second entry is, therefore, an increase in wages in the producer account. The next two entries appear in the consumer account. Income from producers rises by $5 billion, which is the third entry. The fourth entry shows what consumers do with their extra income; if they save all their extra income by increasing their cash balances, personal saving increases. A fifth entry records the purchases in the government account. These purchases were financed by a reduction in government cash balances, which ended up in the hands of consumers. The reduction in government cash balances is recorded as a deficit in the government account, and it is the sixth entry. This completes the circuit. There are six entries in the social accounts, because the transaction involved three parties (government, producers, and consumers), each of which made a double entry.

The social accounts merely record transactions and do not explain why they were made. For example, consumers may want to increase their consumption rather than their cash balances when their income rises. If consumption lags behind income, however, an increase in income would increase cash balances temporarily. An increase in consumer expenditures would produce a second round of changes in the NIA accounts. The behavior of consumers and other sectors is examined in later chapters.

Purchasing sectors with surpluses finance those with deficits. In Table 2–7 only the consumer sector has a surplus; personal saving equals $15 billion. The government, investors, and the rest of the world each ran deficits of $5 billion for a total of $15 billion. On net, consumers acquired financial claims worth $15 billion, which equals the net increase in the debt of the other sectors. In this way the power to purchase goods and services is transferred from one sector to another through financial markets. Financial transactions are reported in the financial flow accounts.

Financial Flow Accounts　The financial flow accounts, which were developed by Professor M. A. Copeland, report the financial transactions of various sectors of the economy. They are sometimes called the money-flow accounts or flow of funds accounts. The accounts in Table 2–8 are simplified and merely illustrate the nature of this accounting system. Six groups of transactors are listed across the top of the table. These groups are derived from the four NIA purchasing sectors by splitting the investor sector into three parts: nonfinancial business, banks, and nonbanks.

Table 2-8 Simplified Financial Flow Accounts, 1972 (billions of dollars)

SOURCES (S) OR USES (U)	CONSUMERS U	CONSUMERS S	GOVERNMENT U	GOVERNMENT S	NONFINANCIAL BUSINESS U	NONFINANCIAL BUSINESS S	BANKS U	BANKS S	NONBANKS U	NONBANKS S	REST OF WORLD U	REST OF WORLD S	TOTAL U	TOTAL S
Surplus or deficit		15	5		5			0		0	5		15	15
Change in financial assets	25		5		10		8		10		5		63	
Change in liabilities		10		10		15		8		10		10		63
Currency and deposits	8		5		−10			8			5		8	8
Bank loans		10				5	20			5			20	20
Government bonds	10			10	8		−8						10	10
Business bonds	2					10	−4		12				10	10
Foreign bonds					12				−2			10	10	10
Life insurance and pensions	5									5			5	5

Banks and nonbanks are both categories of financial institutions. They are treated separately because of their importance in the financial markets. Nonbanks include life insurance companies, trust companies, credit unions, and a large number of other financial institutions, each one of which could be treated as a separate sector. The financial assets and liabilities that are bought and sold in financial markets are listed down the left margin of the table. They include currency and bank deposits; loans by banks; bonds issued by the government, by businesses, and by foreigners; and consumer contributions to life insurance and pension plans. Again, there are a great many other financial claims, such as accounts receivable and common stock, that could be listed, but they are omitted.

The first row of Table 2–8 shows the same surpluses and deficits that appear in Table 2–7 for the NIA purchasing sectors. Consumers had the only surplus, while government, nonfinancial business, and the rest of the world all ran deficits. The last column shows that total surpluses equal total deficits. Consumers used their surplus to acquire financial assets, but they also increased their liabilities. The surplus equals the change in financial assets minus the change in liabilities. Deficits equal the change in liabilities minus the change in financial assets. That is,

surplus = change in financial assets − change in
liabilities
deficit = change in liabilities − change in
financial assets

The changes in financial assets and liabilities that appear in Table 2–8 are the difference between the opening and closing balance sheet items for each sector. Changes in financial assets appear as a use of funds, though the change may be negative; and changes in liabilities appear as a source of funds, which may also be negative. For example, nonfinancial business decreased its currency and demand deposits (a negative use), and it also borrowed from banks (a source), among other transactions. Since there is a debtor and a creditor (buyer and seller) for each IOU, the increase in each liability equals the increase in financial assets in the last column. The changes record only the net flow of financial items from one sector to another, not the total volume of transactions. Consumer cash balances change millions of times during a year, but only the net change from the first to the last day of the year is reported. The net change reports how the surplus or deficit is financed.

Consumers used their surplus of funds to increase their cash balances, to purchase government and business bonds, and to contribute to life insurance and pensions. At the same time they borrowed from banks, but their financial assets increased more than their liabilities. The sectors that ran deficits raised funds either directly from consumers or indirectly by way of financial institutions. For example, nonfinancial business borrowed $5 billion from banks and issued $10 billion in bonds, most of which were purchased by nonbanks. Neither banks nor nonbanks had inside funds of their own but had to raise funds elsewhere. Nonbanks received life insurance and pension contributions from consumers and borrowed from banks, in addition to selling off some foreign bonds. Banks received additional deposits and sold off some bonds. The methods that are available to finance a deficit are practically endless, but ultimately all deficits are financed by surpluses.

The financial flow accounts can be used to answer a number of puzzling questions. First, the financial channels by which personal saving finances business investment in plant and equipment are obvious when consumers buy corporate bonds or when consumers deposit money in banks, which in turn make loans to business, but these channels are not so clear in other cases. Suppose consumers were misers who buried the money they saved in their backyards. How could personal saving then finance investment? Simple. The investor sector could reduce its cash balances in order to buy new plant and equipment from the producer sector. The producer sector could use the same cash to pay the miserly consumer sector for the labor and other factor services that were used to make the new capital goods. Ultimately, consumer cash balances increase by the same amount that business cash balances decrease. Second, newspapers often speak as though people save money, which implies that a positive amount of personal saving requires an increase in the quantity of money. However, consumers can acquire other financial assets or reduce their liabilities. Indeed, most consumer savings are in the form of pensions and life insurance rather than money. Third, during the last few decades the amount of consumer debt in the form of charge accounts, automobile loans, and mortgages has increased tremendously. Does this mean that consumers face ultimate disaster? Some may, but most do not, because personal saving is generally positive. A positive amount of personal saving means that the financial assets of consumers have increased even more than their debt.

Banks and nonbanks do not affect GNP directly, but only indirectly by influencing the behavior of purchasing sectors. They are *financial intermediaries,* which receive funds from surplus sectors and lend funds to deficit sectors. An increase in the quantity of money should not be confused with an increase in spending. They are not the same thing. An increase in the quantity of money may induce one or another sector to increase its spending, but this complicated subject is left to other chapters.

Balance-of-Payments Account   The balance-of-payments account records both financial and nonfinancial transactions between the home country and the rest of the world. It contains no information that is not available in the rest of the world accounts in the national income and financial flow systems; but, unlike those accounts, it is constructed from the point of view of the home country and not the rest of the world. Thus, exports are a source and imports a use of funds.

In the balance-of-payments account, Table 2–9, exports and imports are subdivided into merchandise and services. Services are sometimes called "invisibles" and include shipping, insurance, banking, travel, and interest and dividends—interest and dividends being payments for factor services. International transfer payments are in the nature of gifts; no good, service, or IOU is given in exchange for them. They include funds that immigrants send home and aid to foreign governments. Private and government transfers appear separately, because their behavior differs. Capital transactions are either long-term or short-term, depending on the life of the financial claim. Direct investment, which occurs when a business from one country acquires plant and equipment in another country, is counted as a long-term capital transaction along with IOUs maturing a year or more into the future. Short-term capital transactions include cash balances

Table 2-9   Balance of Payments, 1973 (billions of dollars)

USES		SOURCES	
Current account:		Current account:	
Imports:		Exports:	
Merchandise	17	Merchandise	20
Services	3	Services	5
Transfers:		Transfers:	
Private	3	Private	1
Government	5	Government	0
Capital account:		Capital account:	
Long-term	2	Long-term	− 4
Short-term	−6	Short-term	1
Change in official reserves	−1		
Total uses	23	*Total sources*	23

as well as IOUs due within the year; examples are time deposits, Treasury bills, trade accounts, and commercial paper. Official reserves are the claims that the government or its central bank hold on other countries. They may be U.S. dollars, some other convertible currencies, gold, or net claims on the International Monetary Fund (IMF)—a multinational financial agency. Gold is treated as a financial claim, even though it is a physical asset, because other countries accept it as a claim.

Like the other accounts studied, total sources equal total uses for the balance of payments; yet, there may be a surplus or deficit for any subtotal. If merchandise exports exceed merchandise imports, a surplus—sometimes called a "favorable balance"—exists on *trade account*. If net exports of goods and services plus net transfers are positive, a surplus on *current account* exists. Similar balances can be struck after long-term capital or after short-term capital. Each surplus (deficit) balance has a different significance. Since net exports are a component of aggregate demand, an increase in net exports means an increase in production. A deficit through the short-term capital account means the government has to draw upon its official reserves, so that the change in official reserves is negative.

U.S. Gross National Product

The U.S. gross national product account for 1971 is reproduced in Table 2–10; a complete description is available from the U.S. Department of Commerce. The four components of aggregate demand on the sources side show more detail than Table 2–7 but are otherwise the same. More detailed subcategories are also published. The uses side of the account arranges income to persons, taxes to government, and inside funds differently from Table 2–7 and shows a number of minor items previously omitted. Income to persons includes the following: compensation of employees, proprietors' income, rental income, net interest, dividends, and business transfer payments. Business transfer payments include donations to nonprofit institutions by producers and bad debts of persons. Only taxes paid by producers to government appear; they include corporate profits taxes and indirect business taxes such as the property tax on a factory. Subsidies paid to private enterprises less the net income (profit) of government-owned business-type enterprises also involve the government. Inside funds include undistributed corporate profits, capital consumption, and inventory valuation adjustment. The inventory valuation adjustment is made because businesses do not always use current market prices to value their inventories;

Table 2-10   U.S. Gross National Product, 1971 (billions of dollars)

USES			SOURCES		
Compensation of employees:			Personal consumption expenditures:		
Wages and salaries	573.5		Durable goods	103.5	
Supplements to wages and salaries	70.7		Nondurable goods	278.1	
		644.1	Services	283.3	
Proprietors' income:					664.9
Business and professional	52.6		Gross private domestic investment:		
Farm	17.3		Fixed investment:		
		70.0	Nonresidential	105.8	
Rental income of persons		24.5	Residential	42.6	
Net interest		38.5	Change in inventories	3.6	
Corporate profits before tax:					152.0
Corporate profits tax liability	37.3		Government purchases of goods and services:		
Dividends	25.4		Federal	97.8	
Undistributed profits	20.5		State and local	135.0	
		83.3			232.8
Inventory valuation adjustment		− 4.7	Net exports of goods and services:		
National Income		855.7	Exports	66.1	
Indirect business taxes		101.9	Imports	65.4	
Business transfer payments		4.6			0.7
Subsidies less current surplus of government enterprises		− 0.9			
Statistical discrepancy		− 4.8			
Net National Income		956.6			
Capital consumption allowance		93.8			
Gross National Income		1,050.4	*Gross National Product*		1,050.4

Source: U.S. Department of Commerce, *Survey of Current Business*, 25 (December 1972), pp. 11–12. Some subtotals contain rounding errors.

they sometimes use the prices paid in previous periods, so that inventory investment is sometimes overvalued and sometimes undervalued in terms of current prices. Since GNP measures total output valued at current market prices, this adjustment, which is an adjustment to profits, is necessary to balance the account. The statistical discrepancy arises because the two sides of the account are estimated separately.

Gross national product minus capital consumption equals net national income, or net national product (NNP). NNP is the total amount of new output available during the year after deducting the capital consumed in production. National income is the total payments to the factors of production—land, labor, and capital. Other payments are included in the price of goods but do not go to these factors.

      Figure 2–1 graphs GNP per capita in constant dollars for the United States, the United Kingdom, Japan, Germany, and Canada from 1953 to 1969. Japan had the fastest rate of growth, while the United Kingdom had the slowest. GNP is expressed in constant dollars to eliminate inflation and in per capita terms to reflect the growth in economic welfare of the average person. The 1963 exchange rate is used to express other currencies in terms of the dollar. While GNP is used as an index of economic well-being, it is an imperfect index. It measures total output without respect to what kinds of goods are produced: a dollar's worth of bombs counts as much as a dollar's worth of food. It also does not take account of the exhaustion of natural

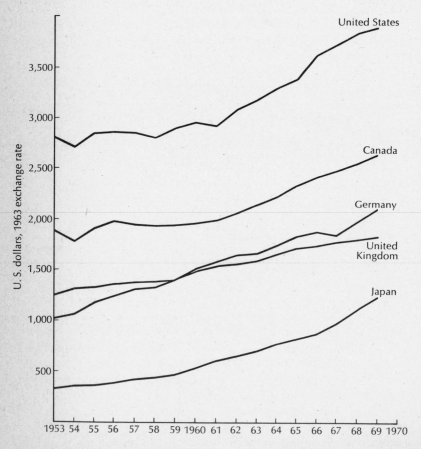

Figure 2-1   GNP per Capita

resources and the pollution of the environment that accompany production and affect the future of mankind.

The gross national product data were originally published to monitor the course of the *business cycle*. The economy goes through periods of prosperity and depression, which occur irregularly and are called cyclical. This irregular up and down movement of GNP appears clearly in the case of the United States in Figure 2–1. Depressions occurred in 1954, 1958, and 1961, while most other years were more prosperous. The other countries had somewhat different cyclical patterns; Japan had no depressions at all—only its rate of growth fluctuated.

The social accounts provide a framework that can be used to construct a model of the economy. GNP equals consumption, government purchases, gross investment, and net exports; but it does not explain what determines the volume of output. Chapter 3 on consumption, Chapter 4 on investment, Chapter 5 on government, and Chapter 6 on foreign trade explain the behavior of the four purchasing sectors; and together they explain the determination of GNP. The influence of finance on the purchasing sectors is treated in Chapter 7.

CONSUMPTION 3

The Consumption Function

The *consumption function* explains the consumer expenditure component of aggregate demand. Aggregate consumption is the total expenditure on consumer goods and services by all households during a given period of time. The subjective preferences of individual households lie behind their demand decisions, as discussed in Chapter 1. Given their preferences, the quantity of a particular good that households demand depends upon their income and upon the price of that particular good relative to the price of other goods. Since aggregate consumption is not concerned with the demand for one good relative to another, the aggregate consumption ignores changes in the relative prices of consumer goods. As a first approximation, the total quantity of consumer goods demanded is a function of consumer income alone. Other factors that may affect aggregate consumption are discussed in the last section of this chapter.

Consumer expenditures and income are both measured here in real terms, referred to as *constant dollars*. Constant dollar measurements are obtained by eliminating changes in the average level of market prices. The total expenditure of consumers is obtained by multiplying the price of each product by the quantity purchased and, then, by adding up the amount spent on each type of consumer product. When prices are held constant, changes in total expenditures measure only changes in the quantities purchased. Similarly, the money income of households may rise because of inflation, so that the real purchasing power of households is measured by deflating personal income. Real income equals money income divided by the average level of prices, and real consumption equals total consumer expenditures divided by the average level of prices.

The consumption function indicates that the quantity of consumer goods demanded increases as the real income of households increases, but not by the full amount of the increase in income.

The consumption function shows how much consumers plan to purchase at alternative levels of income in the same way that the demand curve in Chapter 1 shows how much consumers are willing to buy at alternative prices. An example of a consumption function is illustrated in Table 3–1, in which the

Table 3-1   The Consumption Function

INCOME	CONSUMPTION	AVERAGE PROPENSITY TO CONSUME[1]	MARGINAL PROPENSITY TO CONSUME[2]
(billions of constant dollars)			
Y	C	APC	MPC
0	40		
50	70	1.40	.6
100	100	1.00	.6
150	130	.87	.6
200	160	.80	.6
250	190	.76	.6

[1] $APC = C \div Y$.
[2] $MPC =$ change in $C \div$ change in Y.

income (Y) of all households appears in the first column and the corresponding amount of planned consumption expenditures (C) appears in the second column. When the personal income of all households is $100 billion, planned consumption is $100 billion; and, when income rises to $150 billion, planned consumption is $130 billion. Income has increased by $50 billion, but consumption has increased by only $30 billion. At low levels of income, consumption in Table 3–1 exceeds income. For example, workers who find themselves temporarily unemployed with no income continue to buy consumer goods, which they finance by living off their assets or by borrowing. Income usually exceeds consumption; but if income fell to very low levels, the households in Table 3–1 would tend to spend more than their income.

Figure 3–1, which graphs the data in Table 3–1, shows income (Y) in constant dollars on the horizontal axis and planned consumption (C) in constant dollars on the vertical axis. Consumption is assumed to vary continuously with income even though only a few points are listed in Table 3–1. The graph of the consumption function is an Engel curve for all consumer goods. The curve slopes upward to the right, indicating that aggregate consumption behaves like an ordinary good as opposed to an inferior good. Households in the aggregate increase their spending on consumer goods when their income rises, but their spending does not increase as much as their income.

The general nature of the consumption function is supported by empirical evidence, even though the exact relation

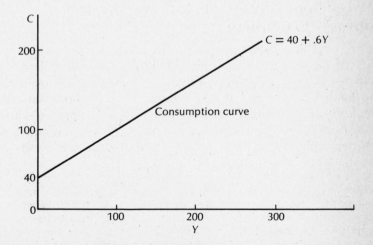

Figure 3-1   The Consumption Function

between income and consumption is not always the same.[1] Cross section data, which report average family income and consumption by income class during a given period of time, indicate that consumption rises less than in proportion to income. As in Table 3–1, the poor tend to spend more than their income, whereas the rich tend to spend less than their income. Cross section studies sometimes show that the consumption curve rises at a diminishing rate at high income levels, that is, as family income increases, spending increases more slowly. Time series data, which report aggregate consumption and income for all households over long periods of time, show that each extra dollar of income is associated with less than a dollar in extra spending, but that consumption tends to remain a constant proportion of income. If personal income goes up by $100 billion, consumption rises by a smaller amount (say, $60 billion), but consumption remains the same percentage (say, 60 percent) of personal income. The consumption curve is a straight line, like Figure 3–1, but it passes through the origin, unlike Figure 3–1.

It may be that consumption curves resemble the cross section data over short periods of time because consumers are responding to what they regard as a temporary situation, while they resemble the time series data over long periods of time. If this is the way consumers behave, consumption will tend to become a larger and larger percentage of income when income declines temporarily; and it will tend to maintain the level of aggregate demand, output, and employment.

Average Propensity to Consume and Marginal Propensity to Consume

The *average propensity to consume (APC)* and the *marginal propensity to consume (MPC)* are also calculated in Table 3–1. The average propensity to consume equals consumption divided by income. Where income is $50 billion and consumption is $70 billion, the average propensity to consume equals 1.40 $(APC = 70 \div 50 = 1.40)$; where income is $150 billion and consumption $130 billion, APC is 0.87. The average propensity to

---

[1] Alternative explanations of the empirical evidence on which the theory of consumption is based may be found in the following: J. S. Duesenberry, *Income, Saving, and the Theory of Consumer Behavior* (Cambridge, Mass.: Harvard University Press, 1949); M. Friedman, *A Theory of the Consumption Function* (Princeton: NBER, 1957); A. Ando and F. Modigliani, "The 'Life Cycle' Hypothesis of Saving: Aggregate Implications and Tests," *American Economic Review*, 53 (March 1963), 55–84.

consume declines in Table 3–1, because consumption increases less than in proportion to income, as cross section studies show.

The marginal propensity to consume equals the change in consumption divided by the change in income. It measures how much extra spending is associated with an extra dollar of income. Where income increases from $50 billion to $100 billion, consumption increases from $70 billion to $100 billion, so that the marginal propensity to consume equals .6 (MPC = change in C ÷ change in Y = 30 ÷ 50 = .6). The marginal propensity to consume is the same throughout Table 3–1. It appears halfway between levels of income, because it measures the change in C between levels of Y.

The consumption function is linear in Figure 3–1 because MPC is constant. This consumption function can, therefore, be depicted by a linear equation:

$$C = 40 + .6Y$$

Where income (Y) is zero, consumption is $40 billion. Graphically, $40 billion is the intercept on the axis measuring consumption. For each extra dollar of income consumption rises by 60 cents. Graphically, .6 is the slope of the consumption function. With this equation, consumption can be calculated for any level of income. At $200 billion in income, consumption equals $40 billion plus .6 times $200 billion, or $160 billion ($C$ = 40 + .6 × 200 = 160).

The Saving Function

The *saving function* describes the same relation as the consumption function, but from a different point of view. In the simple case where personal taxes are not taken into account, personal income (Y) is either spent on consumer goods (C) or is saved (S); and the social account for the household sector can be represented by the following budget equation:

$$Y = C + S$$

If consumption increases 60 cents for every extra dollar of income, the other 40 cents is saved, so that saving as well as consumption varies with income.

The amount of saving is calculated in Table 3–2 on the assumption that the consumption function is the same as that presented in Table 3–1. At low levels of income where planned consumption exceeds income, planned saving is negative. Negative saving is called dissaving. Where income is $50 billion and consumption is $70 billion a year, dissaving is $20 bil-

Table 3-2   The Saving Function

INCOME	CONSUMPTION	SAVING[1]	AVERAGE PROPENSITY	MARGINAL PROPENSITY
	(billions of constant dollars)		TO SAVE[2]	TO SAVE[3]
Y	C	S	APS	MPS
0	40	−40	—	
50	70	−20	−.40	.4
100	100	0	.00	.4
150	130	20	.13	.4
200	160	40	.20	.4
250	190	60	.24	.4

[1] $S = Y - C$.
[2] $APS = S \div Y$.
[3] $MPS =$ change in $S \div$ change in Y.

lion a year. Households are either living off their assets, which is common for retired people, or they are borrowing funds, which is common for young families buying their first automobiles and appliances. At higher levels of income saving is positive.

In Figure 3–2 the saving function is derived from the consumption function graphed in Figure 3–1 and the budget equation $(Y = C + S)$. It can also be drawn from the data in Table 3–2. The top part of the diagram presents the same consumption curve as before and, in addition, presents a 45-degree budget line, based on the household budget equation, which shows that income equals consumption plus saving. For every dollar increase in income, the sum of consumption plus saving also increases by a dollar. The difference between income and consumption is saving. Saving is negative (dissaving) at low levels of income and positive at high levels of income. Where the consumption curve crosses the 45-degree line, saving is zero. The bottom part of Figure 3–2 graphs saving as a function of income. Where income equals zero, the intercept shows that dissaving is $40 billion; where income equals consumption, saving is zero; thereafter saving is positive.

The *average propensity to save* (APS) and the *marginal propensity to save* (MPS) appear in the fourth and fifth columns of Table 3–2. The average propensity to save equals saving divided by income. APS is negative, zero, or positive as saving is negative, zero, or positive. The marginal propensity to save equals the change in saving divided by the change in income. Since each extra dollar of income is either consumed or saved, the MPC plus the MPS equals one, that is,

$$1 = MPC + MPS$$

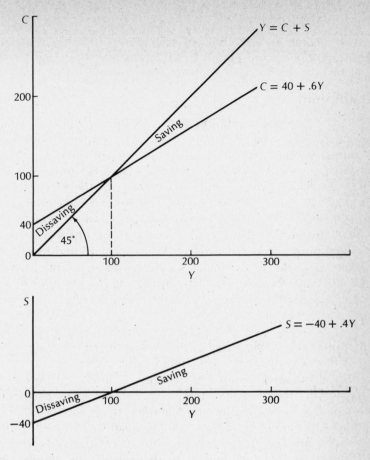

Figure 3-2   The Saving Function

When the *MPC* equals .6, the *MPS* equals .4. The *MPS* is printed between the lines in Table 3–2.

The equation for the saving function in Figure 3–2 is linear like the consumption equation, from which it can be derived.[2] It is composed of an intercept, which measures how much is saved when income is zero, plus the *MPS* (slope) times income.

---

[2] The saving equation can be derived by subtracting the consumption equation from the budget equation.

$$
\begin{array}{rl}
S+C= & Y \\
\text{less:} \quad C= & 40+.6Y \\
\hline
S \quad\;\; = & -40+.4Y
\end{array}
$$

$$S = -40 + .4Y$$

Where income is $200 billion, saving is .4 times $200 billion minus $40 billion and equals $40 billion ($S = -40 + .4 \times 200 = 40$).

Equilibrium

The determination of the equilibrium level of output and income can now be explained with a simplified model of the economy. Suppose the economy is divided into two purchasing sectors: households and all other purchasers. All other purchasers are investors, government, and the rest of the world treated as a single aggregate group. Households demand consumer goods and services (C); all others demand an autonomous quantity (A) of other products. Autonomous means that the quantity of products they purchase is not explained by the simplified model but is taken as given. In particular, autonomous spending (A) does not vary with income (Y). The producing sector allocates to households all of the income (Y) that it receives from selling these two types of products.

In the case of supply and demand, equilibrium exists at that price where the quantity that demanders are willing to buy equals the quantity that suppliers are willing to sell; that is, the quantity demanded equals the quantity supplied. In the case of aggregate demand, equilibrium exists at that level of income where planned spending by all purchasers equals income. Planned spending, or aggregate demand, is the quantity of products that purchasers are willing to buy at alternative levels of income. Equilibrium exists when aggregate demand equals income, because at that point the amount of income received equals the amount of income on which spending plans were based. When transactions are completed, the social account for the producing sector balances and so do the social accounts for households and for all others. For producers, income (Y) equals consumption (C) plus autonomous spending (A), that is,

$$Y = C + A$$

Since the demand for consumer goods is a function of income and the demand for an autonomous quantity of other goods is given, it is possible to determine the equilibrium level of income in Table 3–3, the first two columns of which reproduce the consumption function from Table 3–1. In the third column autonomous spending is assumed to be a constant $20 billion at all levels of income. The sum of consumption (C) and autonomous spending (A) appears in the fourth column. Equilibrium

Table 3-3 The Equilibrium Level of Income¹ (billions of constant dollars)

INCOME Y	CONSUMPTION C	AUTONOMOUS SPENDING A	AGGREGATE DEMAND² C+A
0	40	20	60
50	70	20	90
100	100	20	120
150	130	20	**150**
200	160	20	180
250	190	20	210

¹ In equilibrium $Y = C + A$. Equilibrium values are in boldface type.
² Aggregate demand $= C + A$.

exists at $150 billion, for at that point income (Y) equals aggregate demand (C + A).

Market forces establish the equilibrium level of income or production. If consumers received $100 billion in income and planned to spend $100 billion on consumption at the same time that other purchasers planned to spend an additional $20 billion, income would tend to rise, because income is determined by expenditures. Equilibrium would not be $120 billion, however, because consumption is a function of income and rises as income rises. With a marginal propensity to consume of .6, an extra $20 billion in income would increase consumption by $12 billion, at which point a gap still exists between planned spending (100 + 20 + 12 = 132) and income (100 + 20 = 120). When planned spending exceeds income, income tends to rise. Equilibrium exists when there is no longer a gap between planned spending and income, so that income equals aggregate demand. In Table 3–3 this occurs at $150 billion.

The data in Table 3–3 appear graphically in Figure 3–3. The line labeled C is the consumption function, which shows how much households plan to spend at each level of income. Since autonomous spending is the same at all levels of income, aggregate demand can be represented by the line labeled C + A, which shows planned consumption plus a constant amount of autonomous spending at each level of income. The 45-degree line is the social accounting equation, which shows the equilibrium condition—the total expenditures on output equals the income received and distributed by producers. Since each dollar increase in expenditures increases income by a dollar, the accounting equation for producers rises at an angle of 45 degrees.

The equilibrium level of income is determined by the point where the aggregate demand line (C + A) crosses the 45-

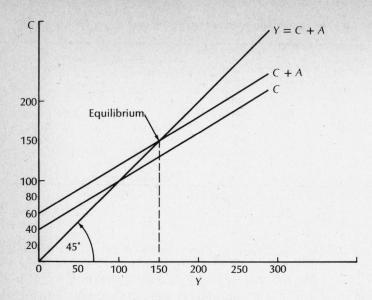

Figure 3-3   The Equilibrium Level of Income

degree line. This occurs at $150 billion. Where income equals $200 billion, equilibrium can not exist because planned spending is only $180 billion. Aggregate demand is insufficient to generate that level of income. The only level of income that simultaneously generates an equal volume of spending is $150 billion.

This simple economy can be represented by a model of three simultaneous equations: (1) a social accounting equation stating the economic necessity that realized income equals actual spending, (2) a consumption equation showing the behavioral relation between income and consumption, and (3) an equation defining the level of autonomous spending.

$$Y = C + A \qquad \text{Social account}$$
$$C = 40 + .6Y \qquad \text{Consumption function}$$
$$A = 20 \qquad \text{Autonomous spending}$$

These equations can be solved by substituting the second and third into the first,

$$Y = 40 + .6Y + 20$$

by subtracting .6Y from both sides,

$$.4Y = 60$$

and, finally, by dividing both sides by .4,

$$Y = 150$$

which gives the equilibrium level of income. Substituting Y back into the consumption equation gives the equilibrium level of consumption:

$$C = 40 + .6(150)$$
$$= 40 + 90$$
$$= 130$$

Whether the equilibrium level of income and consumption is determined numerically as in Table 3–3, graphically as in Figure 3–3, or algebraically as above, the results are the same. More complicated models can not be solved using a table, however, and graphic solutions are also limited, so that mathematics becomes increasingly important as the model becomes larger and more realistic.

The Multiplier

The multiplier measures how much income changes in response to a change in autonomous spending. Income tends to increase by a multiple of an increase in autonomous spending. Considered by itself, an increase in autonomous spending increases income by an equal amount; but, since consumption is a function of income, consumption spending increases as well. For example, suppose the government constructs a $10-million housing project. Income goes up by $10 million in the first instance as contractors, laborers, and suppliers are paid for their services and materials. These contractors, laborers, and suppliers in turn spend a part of their new income on groceries, clothing, and other consumer goods. The amount of the new income they spend is determined by their marginal propensity to consume. This new consumption spending increases the income of grocers, clothiers, and others, who also increase their consumption as their income rises, so that the total increase in income generated by the housing project is greater than $10 million.

The multiplier (k) is defined as *the change in income* (Y) *per dollar change in autonomous spending* (A). That is,

$$k = \frac{\text{change in } Y}{\text{change in } A}$$

The multiplier is denoted by k in recognition of its originator, the British economist R. F. Kahn, who used the concept to explain the impact of public housing construction on employment.

Table 3–4 illustrates what happens to the equilibrium level of income when autonomous spending increases from $20 to $40 billion. The first four columns are the same as in Table 3–3; autonomous spending (A_1) is $20 billion, and the old equilibrium is $150 billion. The fifth column lists the new amount of autonomous spending (A_2) as $40 billion at each level of income. The last column gives the new aggregate demand ($C + A_2$) at each

Table 3-4 The Multiplier[1] (billions of constant dollars)

INCOME Y	CONSUMPTION C	FIRST LEVEL OF AUTONOMOUS SPENDING A_1	FIRST LEVEL OF AGGREGATE DEMAND $C+A_1$	SECOND LEVEL OF AUTONOMOUS SPENDING A_2	SECOND LEVEL OF AGGREGATE DEMAND $C+A_2$
0	40	20	60	40	80
50	70	20	90	40	110
100	100	20	120	40	140
150	130	20	**150**	40	170
200	160	20	180	40	**200**
250	190	20	210	40	230

[1] Equilibrium values are in boldface type.

level of income. The new equilibrium, where planned consumption ($160 billion) plus autonomous spending ($40 billion) equals income, is $200 billion. The multiplier (k) is 2.5, because income increased $50 billion because of a $20-billion increase in autonomous spending ($k = 50 \div 20 = 2.5$). The increase in consumption of $30 billion is called *induced* consumption.

The old ($C + A_1$) and the new ($C + A_2$) aggregate demand curves are plotted in Figure 3–4. The 45-degree line, which shows that actual spending equals realized income in equilibrium, is the same as in Figure 3–3. The old equilibrium level of income is $150 billion. When autonomous spending increases by $20 billion, aggregate demand exceeds income. Therefore, income rises and so does consumption. The new equilibrium level of income ($200 billion) is greater than the old equilibrium ($150 billion) by more than the $20-billion increase in autonomous spending, because consumption is induced to rise $30 billion. Induced consumption is determined by the slope of the consumption function, that is, by the marginal propensity to consume.

The size of the multiplier depends on the size of the marginal propensity to consume. Income changes by the amount of the change in autonomous spending plus the amount of induced consumption. Induced consumption varies directly with the marginal propensity to consume. The larger the marginal propensity to consume, the greater is the proportion of each extra dollar of income that households devote to consumption; thus, the larger the marginal propensity to consume (the steeper the slope of the aggregate demand curve), the greater is the multi-

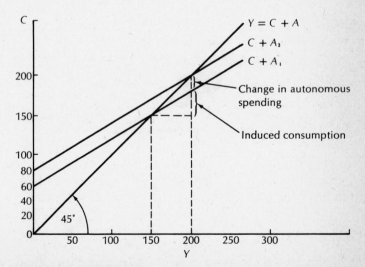

Figure 3-4 The Multiplier

plier. The mathematical relation between the multiplier (k) and the marginal propensity to consume (MPC) is as follows[3]:

$$k = \frac{1}{1-MPC}$$

Where the marginal propensity to consume is .6, the multiplier is 2.5 $[k = 1 \div (1-.6) = 1 \div .4 = 2.5]$. Where $MPC = .8$, $k = 5.0$ $[k = 1 \div (1-.8) = 1 \div .2 = 5.0]$. The multiplier equation can also be written as $k = 1 \div MPS$, since the $MPS = 1 - MPC$. The multiplier is positive, because the marginal propensity lies between zero and one.

During the Great Depression of the 1930s J. M. Keynes proposed that autonomous spending in the form of public works be used to combat unemployment.[4] For every dollar that the government spent on roads, buildings, dams, and so on, output and income would increase by the amount of the multiplier. Employment would be increased and unemployment reduced by more than the number of laborers engaged on public works. As construction workers were paid, their spending would in turn become someone else's income. The employment of a cement worker on a dam, for example, would give rise to the employment of an automobile worker if the cement worker bought a

---

[3] The mathematical relation between the multiplier and the marginal propensity to consume (MPC) can be derived as follows: Let the Greek letter Δ (delta) denote a change in quantity. Using this new symbol, the multiplier is written

$$k = \frac{\Delta Y}{\Delta A}$$

A change in income (ΔY) is composed of two parts: a change in consumption (ΔC) and a change in autonomous spending (ΔA). Thus,

$$\Delta Y = \Delta C + \Delta A$$

Subtracting ΔC from both sides gives

$$\Delta A = \Delta Y - \Delta C$$

Substituting this into the multiplier equation obtains

$$k = \frac{\Delta Y}{\Delta Y - \Delta C}$$

$$= \frac{1}{1 - \frac{\Delta C}{\Delta Y}}$$

$$= \frac{1}{1 - MPC}$$

[4] J. M. Keynes, *The General Theory of Employment, Interest, and Money* (London: Macmillan, 1936).

car. All the government had to do was "prime the pump" in order to bring production back up to the full employment level.

This attractive proposal required two important qualifications. First, once government spending was increased, it had to remain at its new high level. If the government reduced spending to its old level, a multiple contraction in aggregate demand would occur and unemployment would return. The multiplier applies to both increases and decreases in autonomous spending and not, as the pump priming analogy implies, to increases alone. Second, an increase in autonomous spending takes time to affect consumption, because there is a lag in the response of households to an increase in their income. The multiplier presented in Table 3–4 and Figure 3–4 is called an *instantaneous* multiplier because it ignores the period of time necessary for induced consumption to occur. The so-called *period* multiplier is more realistic.

The period multiplier illustrated in Table 3–5 and Figure 3–5 assumes that households make their consumption decisions in one period on the basis of their income in the preceding period. The consumption function is the same as that in Table 3–4 except that it includes a time lag. Starting at an initial equilibrium point where consumption is $130 billion, autonomous spending $20 billion, and income $150 billion, an increase in autonomous spending to $40 billion in the second period increases income to $170 billion, that is, income increases by the

Table 3.5   The Period Multiplier

TIME[1]	CONSUMPTION[2]	AUTONOMOUS SPENDING[3] (billions of constant dollars)	INCOME[4]
t	C	A	Y
1	130.0	20	150.0
2	130.0	40	170.0
3	142.0	40	182.0
4	149.2	40	189.2
5	153.5	40	193.5
6	156.1	40	196.1
—	—	—	—
—	—	—	—
—	—	—	—
n	160.0	40	200.0

[1] Time is measured from the first period ($t=1$) to the last ($t=n$), where n is very large.
[2] Consumption in one period is a function of income in the previous period. For example, in period 3, $C = 40 + .6(170) = 142$.
[3] Autonomous spending is increased to $40 in period 2.
[4] $Y = C + A$ in each period.

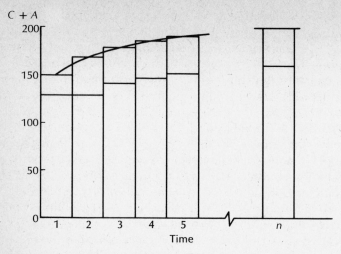

Figure 3-5   The Period Multiplier

amount of the increase in autonomous spending only. Consumption remains at $130 billion, because it is based on an income of $150 billion in the previous period. In the third period, however, consumption rises to $142 billion in response to the rise in income in the second period. Income is now $182 billion. The higher level of income induces a greater amount of consumption in each successive period. The increase in consumption is determined by the marginal propensity to consume. If a sufficient number of periods are allowed to pass, the ultimate equilibrium levels of consumption, autonomous spending, and income will be the same as in the case of the instantaneous multiplier. In Figure 3–5, total spending $(C+A)$ in constant dollars is measured along the vertical axis, time along the horizontal axis.

Other Factors Affecting Consumption

Factors besides income may affect consumption and, therefore, may need to be included in the consumption function. Three such factors are discussed in this section: interest rates, price expectations, and consumer cash balances. Extensive empirical research is necessary to determine whether any or all these factors explain a significant portion of the variation in consumer expenditures. When these other factors change, they may shift the consumption curve up or down.

Interest Rates   Classical economists such as Adam Smith and David Ricardo thought that saving was a function of the rate of interest.[5] They viewed the rate of interest as a reward for saving: the higher the rate of interest, the larger the volume of saving. Since what is not saved is consumed, an increase in the interest rate, which brings forth an increased volume of saving, reduces the amount of consumption. Thus, the classical economists implicitly thought that consumption was inversely related to the rate of interest.

J. M. Keynes criticized the classical theory on the grounds that Adam Smith, David Ricardo, and their followers supposed that the main motive for saving was to provide for a greater amount of future consumption—if not for one's self, then for one's heirs. Households were supposed to reduce their present consumption when the interest rate increased, in the expectation that their future consumption would be increased by more than enough to compensate them for their present sacrifice. Keynes observed that households may save in order to provide themselves with a given annuity or retirement income. If consumers desire to have a given income per year at some future date, they do not need to save as much at high interest rates as they do at low interest rates. At a high interest rate their wealth will increase faster and will yield a larger income than at a low interest rate. Thus, saving could be inversely related to the rate of interest. Keynes concluded that, in any event, the rate of interest does not have much influence on saving or consumption.

Price Expectations Household expectations about the future course of prices may affect their present consumption expenditures. When households expect the average level of prices to rise, they are better off buying now rather than later. If they wait, they will only be able to buy a smaller quantity of consumer goods with the same money income. Conversely, the expectation of falling prices may lead consumers to reduce their present consumption in hopes of buying goods more cheaply in the future.

Price expectations may tend to destabilize the economy, especially in periods of rapid inflation. When prices are rising very rapidly, consumers may spend their incomes as soon as possible in order to acquire as much as possible in real goods and services. The demand for goods and services would be, therefore, increased beyond what it would have been in the absence of inflation; thus, excess demand in general would be increased

---

[5] The views of these authors can be found in Adam Smith, *The Wealth of Nations* (New York: Modern Library, 1937), and David Ricardo, *The Principles of Political Economy and Taxation*, P. Sraffa, ed. (Cambridge: Cambridge University Press, 1951), vol. 1.

and the price rise accelerated. Under these conditions rapid inflation breeds even more rapid inflation.

Consumer Cash Balances   A. C. Pigou, Don Patinkin, and others argue that the real value of cash balances affects consumption.[6] If cash balances are sufficiently large, the motive to save is reduced; therefore, households with large cash balances spend more than households with the same income but with lower cash balances. The real value of cash balances is measured by the dollar value of cash balances divided by the average level of prices. Since it is the real value of cash balances that affects consumption, price changes indirectly affect consumption. A fall in prices increases real cash balances so that households become richer, save less, and consume more.

The effect of real cash balances on consumption tends to stabilize the economy when prices are flexible. This is called the *Pigou effect*. In particular, a general excess supply of output tends to reduce product prices. As the price level falls, given the dollar value of cash balances held by households, the real value of cash balances increases, and in turn consumption increases. To be somewhat fanciful, when a new car costs a dime, the demand for new cars will be immense, given the number of dimes in circulation. Thus, a fall in the average level of prices, if it proceeded far enough, ought to increase consumption and production and thereby tend to eliminate unemployment. The Pigou effect is of little practical importance, in part because prices do not decline during periods of general excess supply and in part because it would be simpler and quicker to increase real cash balances by increasing the number of dollars in circulation.

---

[6] A. C. Pigou, "The Classical Stationary State," *Economic Journal*, 53 (December 1943), 343–351; and Don Patinkin, *Money, Interest, and Prices*, 2d ed., (New York: Harper and Row, 1965).

4

INVESTMENT

Investment Defined

Investment is the second component of aggregate demand, the demand for newly produced capital goods. Capital goods are real physical goods. For example, a factory or machine is a capital good for a producer; a house is a capital good for a consumer; and a highway is a government capital good. Capital goods are the only factor of production produced by the factors of production—land, labor, and capital. The accumulation or stock of capital goods that exists at the end of an accounting period can be used to produce future goods and services: factories manufacture goods, houses serve their occupants, and highways serve the public. An inventory of goods and materials is capital, even though it may be perishable, because it can satisfy wants in the near or distant future.

Gross investment is the quantity of newly produced capital goods acquired during a period of time, say, a year. If gross investment exceeds the amount of capital consumption during a year, there is a net addition to the capital stock. Capital consumption includes accidental destruction and obsolescence as well as ordinary wear and tear, because all three elements reduce the value of the capital stock. When a greater quantity of capital goods exists at the end of a year than at the beginning, *net* investment has occurred. Net investment equals gross investment minus capital consumption; that is, net investment equals the change in the capital stock. A decline in the stock of capital goods is called *disinvestment*.

For example, if an automobile rental company acquires 20 new cars of the same type at the same cost each year, its annual gross investment equals the value of 20 new cars; but if each car lasts only five years, the company will never have more than 100 cars. When the 20 new cars that are purchased each year merely replace those that wear out, the annual net investment of the company is zero. Depreciation is an approximate measure of the decline in value of a stock of capital goods. In this example, it would be reasonable to assume that the value of each car declines by one-fifth of its original cost each year, though in the marketplace it may depreciate more rapidly when it is new than when it is old.

The following section considers only the demand for capital goods by productive enterprises, which are assumed to maximize their profits. Consumers and governments act on other principles. The obsolescence of capital goods that arises from technical progress is ignored so that the quantity of capital can be measured in constant dollars. If the same sum of money measured in constant dollars purchases a more productive machine today than it purchased a decade ago, constant dollars would not accurately reflect the value of the capital stock.

Investment Demand

Investment demand by producers follows the law of demand, because the rate of return on capital declines as a greater quantity of capital is accumulated. This occurs for two reasons. First, output increases at a diminishing rate as additional units of capital are taken into production, provided other factors of production are fixed, because of the law of diminishing returns. Second, the output attributable to an additional unit of capital is produced over the life of the capital good; and, since output that is produced in the future is not worth as much to the businessman as output that is available today, future returns are discounted by him. Each of these reasons is discussed in turn, and then they are combined to explain the demand for capital goods.

Capital and Diminishing Returns   Chapter 1 presented the law of diminishing returns in the case where labor was the variable input. The same law applies to capital. However, the relation of output to capital varies from one type of capital good to another, so each type of capital good must be considered separately. As additional units of one type of capital enter production, output increases at a diminishing rate, provided the quantity of other inputs remains fixed. The fixed inputs could be other types of capital goods as well as land and labor.

In Table 4–1 capital is measured in physical units of a particular type of capital good, such as railroad cars. Each unit will be assumed to cost the same amount, $100 in constant dollars. Output in the second column is measured in constant dollars, which in the simplest case represents a particular type of output valued at a constant price. Since each different type of capital good has its own relation to output, separate tables would have to be constructed for different capital goods. A profit-maximizing enterprise purchases that combination of capital goods which produces the greatest possible output for a given expenditure.

The value of the marginal product of capital in the third column is the increase in output, measured in constant dol-

Table 4-1   Value of the Marginal Product of Capital

CAPITAL INPUT (units)	OUTPUT (constant dollars)	VALUE OF THE MARGINAL PRODUCT (constant dollars)
0	0	
		250
1	250	
		200
2	450	
		150
3	600	
		100
4	700	
		50
5	750	

lars, that is associated with an extra unit of capital. It is produced over the whole life of the capital good, whether that be two or twenty years. The first unit of capital increases output from zero to $250, so its marginal product is $250; the second unit adds $200 to output, which is its marginal product. The value of the marginal product declines from $250 to $200 to $150 and so on because of the law of diminishing returns.

Discounting Future Returns Discounting future returns is another way of looking at compound interest, which is more familiar. A person who lends a sum of money, which is called his *principal*, for a period of time generally expects to be repaid his principal plus interest, otherwise he would not part with his money. If the interest that is due at the end of the period is computed on the original principal, it is called *simple* interest. For example, if a person lends $100 for one year at 10 percent per year, he expects to receive at the end of the year his $100 principal plus $10 simple interest, or $110 in all. If a loan is for more than one period and if the interest due at the end of each period is added to the principal for the purpose of computing the interest in subsequent periods, the amount due at the end of the last period is the original principal plus *compound* interest. If $100 is lent for two years at 10 percent per year compounded annually, it earns 10 percent of $100 for the first year plus 10 percent of $110 for the second year, so that $121 is due at the end of the second year.

The formula for compound interest can be developed intuitively. Let P_0 be the initial principal and i be the rate of interest; then, the amount of money due at the end of the first period (P_1) is

$$P_1 = P_0 + iP_0$$
$$= (1+i)P_0$$

If the principal is lent for two periods at compound interest, the amount due at the end of the second period (P_2) is

$$P_2 = (1+i)P_1$$
$$= (1+i)(1+i)P_0$$
$$= (1+i)^2 P_0$$

When $100 is lent for two years at 10 percent compounded annually, a total of $121 is due at the end of the second year [$121 = (1.10)(1.10)100$]. For three periods the formula becomes

$$P_3 = (1+i)P_2$$
$$= (1+i)^3 P_0$$

Therefore, intuition suggests that the formula for compound interest for any number of periods (*t*) is the following:

$$P_t = (1 + i)^t P_0$$

where P_0 is the original principal, P_t is the amount due at the end of the last period, *i* is the rate of interest, and *t* is the number of periods.

Discounting turns around the problem of compound interest. Instead of asking, "How much will an initial sum of money be worth in so many years compounding at a certain rate of interest?", discounting asks, "How much is a final sum of money due so many years in the future worth today, discounting at a given rate of interest?" Compound interest and discounting are compared in Table 4–2. On the one hand, if $62.09 is lent at

Table 4-2   Compound Interest[1] and Discounting

	COMPOUND INTEREST		DISCOUNTED PRESENT VALUE
Original principal	$ 62.09	Present value	$ 62.09
Year 1	68.30		68.30
2	75.13		75.13
3	82.64		82.64
4	90.90		90.90
5	100.00		100.00
Compound value	$100.00	*Amount due*	$100.00

[1] Interest is assumed to compound at 10 percent per annum.

10 percent for five years, it will compound to $100 at the end of five years. On the other hand, if $100 is due in five years and the rate of discount is 10 percent, its present value is $62.09. The original principal in the compound interest problem is the same as the present value in the discounting problem. Thus, the formula for the discounted *present value* (P_0) of a given sum of money (P_t) due in *t* years is

$$P_0 = \frac{P_t}{(1 + i)^t}$$

Savings bonds, for example, are sold at their discounted present value. A $100 savings bond is not worth $100 unless it is held to maturity (say, eight years); when it is issued, it sells for less than $100 (say, $75).

The Demand for Capital Goods   The demand for capital goods is determined by the discounted value of the marginal product of capital. The principle of opportunity cost requires that the marginal product of capital be discounted. Instead of investing in a capital good, which yields a stream of income over a number of years in the future, an enterprise has the alternative of lending its funds out at the market rate of interest. If the rate of return from the capital good is greater than the rate of interest from lending funds, it is better off buying the capital good; otherwise it is better off lending its funds, assuming that the income from the capital project and from the loan are equally certain.

An enterprise needs to know how much extra output can be expected from a unit of capital during each year of its life. The discounted present value of the extra output measures the productive worth of the capital good to the enterprise. If the present value of the marginal product of capital at a given rate of discount exceeds the cost of the capital good, the enterprise can expect to earn at least that rate of discount when it acquires the capital good.

Table 4-3   Discounting the Value of the Marginal Product of Capital[1]

VALUE OF THE MARGINAL PRODUCT	PRESENT VALUE AT VARIOUS RATES OF DISCOUNT						
	10%	20%	30%	40%	50%	60%	70%
$250	$207	$176	$151	$132	$117	$105	$95
200	166	140	121	105	94	84	76
150	124	105	91	79	70	63	57
100	83	70	61	53	47	42	38
50	41	35	30	26	23	21	19

[1] Each unit of capital costs $100, lasts three years, and produces an equal output each year.

The first column in Table 4–3 shows the undiscounted value of the marginal product of capital from Table 4–1. The other columns show the present value of the marginal product at various rates of discount, assuming that the life of the capital good is three years and that it produces an equal output in each year of its life.[1] For example, the marginal product of the first unit of capital is $250, or a net income of $83.33 for each of three years. The net income of $83.33 due in one year is worth $75.75 today when it is discounted at 10 percent; that is, $75.75 invested at 10 percent is worth $83.33 at the end of one year (75.75 + 7.58

[1] The scrap value of the capital good at the end of its life is assumed to be zero.

=83.33). The present value of $83.33 due in two years is $68.86 and due in three years is $62.65. Therefore, the stream of income of $83.33 a year for all three years discounted at 10 percent has a present value of $207.27, which is calculated as follows:

$$207.27 = \frac{83.33}{(1.10)} + \frac{83.33}{(1.10)^2} + \frac{83.33}{(1.10)^3}$$

$$= \frac{83.33}{1.10} + \frac{83.33}{1.21} + \frac{83.33}{1.33}$$

$$= 75.75 + 68.87 + 62.65$$

$$= 207.27$$

Since the capital good costs $100 a unit, the present value of the marginal product discounted at 10 percent exceeds the cost of the good; and the enterprise can expect to earn more than 10 percent. Indeed, the present value exceeds the cost until the rate of discount rises past 60 percent, so that the first unit of capital earns at least 60 percent. The second unit of capital produces a smaller marginal product, and its present value is less at each rate of discount. As more units of capital are taken into production, the marginal product declines still further.

The _rate of return_ on a capital good is that rate of discount which equates the expected stream of income with the current cost of the capital good. The stream of income over the entire life of the capital good is the value of the marginal product of capital. In terms of the present value formula, the rate of return (r) equates the annual income (A) with the current cost (C_0) of the capital good:

$$C_0 = \frac{A_1}{(1+r)} + \frac{A_2}{(1+r)^2} + \cdots + \frac{A_t}{(1+r)^t}$$

The approximate rate of return for the example in Table 4–3 appears in Table 4–4. When the value of the marginal product exceeds the cost of the capital good, the rate of return is positive; when they are equal, it is zero; and when the value of the marginal product is less than the cost of the capital good, the rate of return is negative. Like the value of the marginal product, from which it is derived, the rate of return declines as more capital is employed. Keynes called the rate of return the _marginal efficiency of capital_.

The demand curve for a capital good shows the relation between the quantity of capital demanded and the rate of return. Figure 4–1 graphs the data in Table 4–4, except that the capital input is measured in constant dollars at $100 a unit. It

Table 4-4   Rate of Return on Capital

CAPITAL INPUT (units)	VALUE OF THE MARGINAL PRODUCT	RATE OF RETURN[1]
0		
	$250	65%
1		
	200	45
2		
	150	23
3		
	100	0
4		
	50	−28
5		

[1] The rate of return is approximate.

follows the law of demand; that is, the rate of return declines as additional units of capital are acquired. As long as the rate of return on a particular type of capital good is greater than the cost of borrowing funds at the market rate of interest, an enterprise increases its profit by acquiring more capital goods, that is, by investing. It maximizes its profit when the rate of return equals the cost of borrowing, for up to that point its additional revenue exceeds its additional cost.

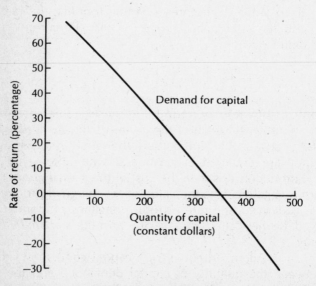

Figure 4-1   The Demand for a Capital Good

When an enterprise uses several different types of capital goods, it maximizes its profit for a given investment by equating the rate of return on each type of capital good. If it could earn a higher rate of return on one type of capital good than another, it would increase its profit by acquiring more units of that capital good with the higher rate of return. When it can no longer increase its profit by reallocating its capital, it has maximized its profit for a given amount of investment.

The demand curve for capital is downward sloping, not only because of the law of diminishing returns, but also because the marginal product of capital is discounted. If two different types of capital goods add the same amount to total revenue and the same amount to total cost over the course of their lives, but if one has a shorter life than the other, the one with the shorter life has the greater rate of return; it takes fewer years to produce the same marginal product. Therefore, as the market rate of interest declines, longer lasting capital goods become more profitable, and the quantity of capital demanded increases.

Investment and the Rate of Interest

At the macroeconomic level the demand for capital is the aggregate of the demand for all the individual types of capital goods.[2] The quantity of newly produced capital goods that is acquired during a period of time is the amount of gross investment. Net investment is gross investment minus the consumption of old capital that is already in place in a fixed form. If no new capital goods are produced, the capital stock declines by the amount of the capital consumption.

Gross investment, capital consumption, and net investment per year at various rates of return appear in Table 4–5. Capital consumption is assumed to be $10 billion, so net investment is $10 billion less than gross investment. As investment increases, the rate of return declines. The investment demand curve in Figure 4–2 relates the data for gross investment to the rate of return; that is, it shows the relation between the quantity of new capital goods that enterprises are willing to purchase during a year and the expected rate of return.

---

[2] The aggregation of individual demand functions for capital goods involves problems that are not solved here. For example, the productiveness of one type of capital good is not independent of the quantity of other capital goods in use; thus, when the quantity of capital in general increases, individual demand functions tend to shift.

Table 4-5   Aggregate Investment Demand

GROSS INVESTMENT	CAPITAL CONSUMPTION (billions of constant dollars)	NET INVESTMENT	RATE OF RETURN (percentage)
0	10	−10	25
10	10	0	20
20	10	10	15
30	10	20	10
40	10	30	5
50	10	40	0

When deciding what quantity of capital goods to purchase, enterprises use the principle of opportunity cost to compare the rate of return on capital goods with the rate of interest in financial markets. If the rate of return exceeds the market rate of interest, enterprises can increase their profits by borrowing funds and buying capital goods. If the rate of interest is above the rate of return, an enterprise would be better off lending any funds that it may possess.

In equilibrium the rate of return on capital goods equals the rate of interest on funds. If the rate of interest is 15 percent in Figure 4–2, for example, enterprises maximize their profits by purchasing $20 billion in new capital goods, of which $10 billion is net investment. Up to $20 billion, profits can be increased by borrowing at a rate below the return on capital. If the rate of interest were to rise to 25 percent (or higher), no

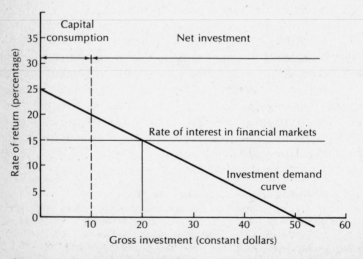

Figure 4-2   Gross Investment Demand

new capital goods would be demanded and the capital stock would decline by $10 billion.

Figure 4–2 is based on two simplifications, which affect the detail, but not the substance, of the analysis. First, there is not a single rate of interest in financial markets, but a complex of interest rates reflecting the different risk, maturity, and liquidity of various IOUs. Second, the risk of investing in capital goods is ignored. These matters are treated in more advanced books.

The equation for the investment demand curve in Figure 4–2 is

$$I = 50 - 2i$$

where I is the volume of investment and i is the rate of interest, which equals the rate of return on capital in equilibrium.[3] When the rate of interest is zero, investment is $50 billion; and, for every percentage point rise in the interest rate, investment declines by $2 billion. At 7 percent, investment is $36 billion [$36 = 50 - 2(7)$].

Saving and Investment

Saving equals investment in an economy where the output of producers is purchased by households in the form of consumer goods and by investors in the form of capital goods. A system of social accounts for such an economy appears in Table 4–6. Consumers receive all the income (Y) generated by production, which they either spend on consumption (C) or save (S). Investment (I) is the final output of producers that is purchased by enterprises with funds (F) raised through financial channels.

The social accounting equations from Table 4–6 show that for producers

$$Y = C + I$$

and for consumers

$$Y = C + S$$

Since saving and investment are both equal to the same thing ($Y - C$), they are equal to each other:

$$S = I$$

---

[3] As was noted earlier, economists sometimes put the dependent variable on the horizontal axis, instead of the other way around.

Table 4-6   An Economy of Consumers and Investors (billions of constant dollars)

	PRODUCERS	
Uses	Sources	
Y 150	C 130	
	I 20	

CONSUMERS				INVESTORS	
Uses	Sources		Uses	Sources	
C 130	Y 150		I 20	F 20	
S 20					

A model of income determination can be developed from the saving and investment equation.

In Chapter 3 saving was shown to be a function of income: the greater the level of income, the more consumers plan to save. The saving function from Figure 3–2 is reproduced in Figure 4–3. Earlier in this chapter, investment was shown to be a function of the rate of interest: the lower the rate of interest, the greater the demand for investment. Figure 4–2 is turned on its side in Figure 4–3, so that both saving and investment are measured vertically up from the origin.

When the rate of interest is 15 percent, investment is $20 billion. Equilibrium is established where saving equals invest-

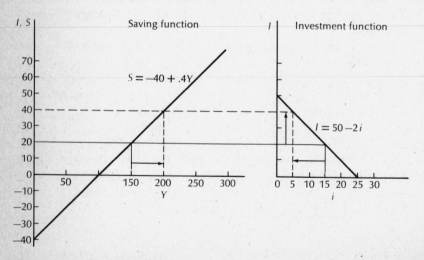

Figure 4-3   Saving and Investment

ment, which is where income equals $150 billion. The remaining quantities in Table 4–6 can also be calculated. If income is $150 billion and investment is $20 billion, consumption must be $130 billion. (These are the same equilibrium quantities obtained in Chapter 3 when autonomous spending was $20 billion.) Notice that the volume of saving is just sufficient to finance investment. In equilibrium every dollar is accounted for, because every dollar spent is received.

If the rate of interest falls to 5 percent, enterprises can increase their profits by purchasing more capital goods, because the new lower rate of interest is below the old rate of return on capital. Investment tends to rise to $40 billion, at which point profits are maximized. However, when investment is $40 billion, it exceeds the amount that consumers plan to save out of an income of $150 billion; but the rise in investment also increases the level of income. As income rises, consumers are induced to increase both their consumption and saving until equilibrium is established at $200 billion, at which point saving is $40 billion. At this new equilibrium point saving is just sufficient to finance investment.

This same model can be presented algebraically in a system of three equations:

$$S = I \qquad \text{Social account}$$
$$S = -40 + .4Y \qquad \text{Saving function}$$
$$I = 50 - 2i \qquad \text{Investment function}$$

where the interest rate (i) is exogenous; that is, it is determined outside of the system. The equilibrium level of income is found by substituting the second and third equations in the first:

$$-40 + .4Y = 50 - 2i$$
$$.4Y = 90 - 2i$$
$$Y = 225 - 5i$$

Where the rate of interest is 15 percent, income is $150 billion; where the interest rate is 5 percent, income is $200 billion.

The decline in the interest rate increases income by more than the increase in investment spending because of the multiplier. When the interest rate falls by 10 percentage points, investment rises by $20 billion and income rises by $50 billion. Therefore, the investment multiplier (k) is 2.5, which equals

$$k = \frac{1}{1 - MPC}$$
$$= \frac{1}{MPS}$$

This simple model does not go very far. It does not explain the determination of the interest rate, which is left until Chapter 7; and it does not include the other two components of aggregate demand, government purchases and net exports, which are discussed in the next two chapters.

The Variability of Investment

Investment fluctuates substantially from year to year and is one of the most variable components of aggregate demand. Two reasons for its variability are discussed in this section: business expectations and the acceleration principle.

Business Expectations   The rate of return on a capital good is estimated from the future returns that can be expected over the course of its life. These expected returns can not be known with certainty; they depend on the subjective evaluations of businessmen. Business expectations are notoriously unstable, as a glance at stock market quotations will confirm. The prices of common stocks frequently change by large amounts when there has been no change in dividends, profits, or other fundamental conditions. These fluctuations are often the result of volatile subjective expectations. Overoptimism creates in the minds of businessmen future returns that may never be realized, and they lead enterprises to buy capital goods that may never be profitable. Pessimism produces the opposite result.

Economists from quite different schools of thought have laid the blame for the variability of investment and the resulting fluctuations in income and employment on the volatile nature of business expectations. T. B. Veblen,[4] who was an institutionalist, A. C. Pigou,[5] who was a neoclassicist, and J. M. Keynes,[6] who laid the foundation for modern macroeconomics, all agreed that waves of optimism and pessimism produce cycles in output and employment.

During recessions businessmen are pessimistic and unwilling to invest in any but the most profitable ventures; even replacement needs may not be met. The revival of production comes when pessimism turns to guarded optimism. Investment rises and produces a multiple increase in income, which reinforces an optimistic view of the future. Optimism brings forth

---

[4] T. B. Veblen, *The Theory of Business Enterprise* (New York: Scribner, 1904).
[5] A. C. Pigou, *Industrial Fluctuations* (London: Macmillan, 1927).
[6] J. M. Keynes, *The General Theory of Employment, Interest, and Money* (London: Macmillan, 1936).

more investment and higher income, so that it tends to be self-justifying. But optimistic plans must eventually be realized or a crisis will occur. Keynes called this a collapse in the marginal efficiency of capital, which leads back to recession and completes the cycle.

Acceleration Principle The acceleration principle was developed by J. M. Clark,[7] among others. It supposes that there is a direct and constant relation between the amount of capital employed and the level of output. When the productive capacity of the economy is fully utilized, the capital stock must increase in order to increase output—there must be investment. If output grows at an increasing rate like compound interest, capital must accumulate at an accelerating rate; that is, investment must be larger each year. Should output grow more slowly, however, investment would decline. With a constant level of output, net investment would be zero.

The acceleration principle can be used to explain the demand for airplanes by airlines. If passenger traffic grows at 10 percent a year, airlines will need 10 percent more airplanes each year, so that the demand for airplanes will grow, too. Airplane manufacturers will need to build larger factories and employ more men in order to meet the demand. However, if passenger traffic stops growing and levels off, there is no need for new airplanes, except to replace those that wear out. Thus, the demand for airplanes will fall drastically, and thousands of people in the airplane industry will be dismissed, even though passenger traffic remains the same year after year.

P. A. Samuelson[8] combined the acceleration principle with the multiplier to show how an economy may go through cycles. If there is a permanent increase in investment, the multiplier increases income in the periods that follow. When consumers receive the extra income from the new investment, they increase their consumption according to their marginal propensity to consume, which is ordinarily less than one. Income again is increased by the amount of the new consumption; and this leads to a further, but smaller, increase in consumption and income, until a new equilibrium is established. However, the increase in consumption induces a greater demand for capital,

---

[7] J. M. Clark, "Business Acceleration and the Law of Demand: A Technical Factor in Economic Cycles," *Journal of Political Economy* 25 (March 1917), 217–235.
[8] P. A. Samuelson, "Interaction between Multiplier Analysis and the Principle of Acceleration," *Review of Economic Statistics* 25 (May 1939), 75–78.

as explained by the acceleration principle. Thus, investment induces more consumption via the multiplier, and consumption induces more investment via the acceleration principle. What ultimately happens? Since consumption rises at a diminishing rate in response to an increase in investment, investment demand may ultimately turn downward, and output may go through a cycle, but this need not occur.[9]

Samuelson's multiplier-accelerator model provides theoretical evidence to support the factual evidence that cyclical fluctuations in output and employment may continue forever, unless the government intervenes. The role of the government in the economy and its effect on aggregate demand are considered in the next chapter.

[9] Samuelson solved this problem using second-order difference equations, which, like so many other topics, is best left to a more advanced text.

GOVERNMENT 5

The Government Sector

The government sector in the national income accounts includes general government activities from the national to the local level, but it excludes government-owned enterprises, ranging from canals to liquor stores, that operate on business principles. The transactions of this complex sector can be classified into sources and uses of funds. The main source of funds is taxes: direct and indirect, corporate and personal. The main uses of funds are purchases of newly produced goods and services (ranging from bilge pumps to bulletin boards) and transfer payments to persons (ranging from aid to dependent children to old-age pensions). When the sources of funds exceed expenditures on output and on transfers, the government budget shows a surplus, which appears as a use of funds in Table 2–7; when expenditures exceed receipts, the budget shows a deficit; and when expenditures equal receipts, the budget is balanced.

This chapter considers the relation between the government budget and aggregate demand. Sections are devoted to purchases of output and taxes on persons, first taken separately and then jointly. The final section considers the purchases, transfers, taxes, and deficits of the government budget as fiscal policy tools for controlling aggregate demand. Fiscal policy is the plan of the government for its budget, and its budget affects aggregate demand. Aggregate demand in its turn affects unemployment, inflation, and the balance of payments, though these three problems are not discussed until later.

Government Purchases

Government purchases of goods and services make up the third component of aggregate demand, following consumption and investment. Since the government directly controls these purchases, it can use them as fiscal policy tools to control the economy. Government purchases are treated as autonomous expenditures that are unrelated to income, even though there are certain types of government purchases that depend on the level of economic activity, such as the relation of highway construction to the number of automobiles.

The effect of autonomous expenditures on income and output has already been discussed in Chapter 3 and will only be reviewed here. Suppose the economy has only two purchasing sectors: consumers and government. In equilibrium, income (Y) equals consumption (C) plus an autonomous amount of government purchases (G). This equilibrium condition is represented by the 45-degree line in Figure 5–1. The consumption function relates the planned purchases of households to personal income: as income increases, consumption increases, but not by the full amount of the increase in income. The marginal propensity to consume is less than one. The consumption function in Figure 5–1 is labeled C. An initial level of government purchases is added to consumption at every level of income to form an aggregative demand curve, which is labeled $C + G_0$.

In equilibrium the total expenditures on output ($C + G_0$) equal the amount of income (Y) that is generated by production. In Figure 5–1 where the initial amount of government purchases is G_0, the equilibrium level of income is Y_0. If govern-

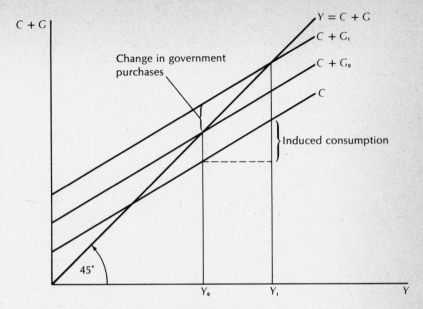

Figure 5-1   Government Purchases and the Multiplier

ment purchases are increased to G_1, income rises by a multiple of the increase in G. In the first instance income is increased directly by the amount of the increase in government purchases; but, since consumption increases as income increases, aggregate demand rises by more than the increase in government purchases. In Figure 5–1 the equilibrium amount of income rises to Y_1, which is greater than the initial equilibrium (Y_0) by the amount of the increase in government purchases plus induced consumption. The multiplier is the same as before:

$$k = \frac{\text{change in income}}{\text{change in government purchases}}$$
$$= \frac{1}{1 - MPC}$$

Government purchases must be financed in some way. Either taxes must be collected or funds raised in financial markets. The government can raise funds in financial markets by increasing its liabilities or by decreasing its financial assets. It usually increases its liabilities (or borrows) by issuing short-term Treasury bills (60 days to one year), intermediate-term notes (up to five years), or long-term bonds. Borrowing to finance purchases is referred to as *deficit financing* or *deficit spending*. When the government finances an increase in its purchases by running a deficit, income increases by the full amount of the multiplier. But if the government increases taxes, households do not have as much to spend on consumption, so that the multiplier is smaller and the multiplier formula differs from that used in the case of deficit spending.

Taxes

The role of taxes in the economy can be illustrated by two types of personal taxes: a *lump sum* tax and an *income* tax. A lump sum tax is a constant amount at all levels of income. The old poll tax, which citizens had to pay in order to vote, and the Pennsylvania occupation tax, which each person has to pay according to his occupation, are examples of lump sum taxes. At least they are lump sum taxes to the extent that they are not very sensitive to changes in GNP; they are income taxes to the extent that the rich pay more than the poor. In the case of the poll tax, the poor could avoid it by not voting, which was its purpose; in the case of the occupation tax, high income occupations generally pay more than low income occupations. The personal income tax is a more obvious example of an income tax.

Taxes enter the consumption function when they are paid by households. Instead of being a function of income alone, consumption (C) becomes a function of income (Y) minus taxes (T), or disposable income ($Y-T$). Households spend what they have left at their disposal after taxes. Thus, the consumption function from Chapter 3 becomes

$$C = 40 + .6(Y - T)$$

For a lump sum tax, T is a constant; for an income tax, T varies with Y. If no taxes are paid, income and disposable income are the same.

Lump Sum Tax   A lump sum tax tends to reduce consumption at every level of income. Table 5-1 presents the consumption

Table 5-1   Consumption and a Lump Sum Tax (billions of constant dollars)

INCOME Y	CONSUMPTION BEFORE TAX C_{before}	TAX T	DISPOSABLE INCOME $(Y-T)$	CONSUMPTION AFTER TAX C_{after}
0	40	50	− 50	10
50	70	50	0	40
100	100	50	50	70
150	130	50	100	100
200	160	50	150	130
250	190	50	200	160

function used in Chapter 3 before and after a lump sum tax of $50 billion. Following the imposition of the tax, disposable income is $50 billion less than income; but consumption is only $30 billion less than it was before the tax, because the marginal propensity to consume is .6. Consumption falls by $30 billion when income falls by $50 billion. Where disposable income was $150 and consumption $130 billion before the tax, they are both $100 billion after the tax.

Figure 5–2 graphs consumption before (C_{before}) and after (C_{after}) the tax as a function of income without the tax. All quantities are measured in billions of constant dollars. The consumption function after the tax is $30 billion below and parallel to the consumption function before the tax, because consumption fell $30 billion at every level of income.

The equilibrium level of income is determined graphically in Figure 5–3 in the case where income is reduced by a lump sum tax. An autonomous amount of government purchases is added to the consumption curves in order to form the aggregate demand curves. The broken lines indicate the consumption and aggregate demand curves before the tax; the solid lines, after the tax. Equilibrium occurs where the aggregate demand curves intersect the 45-degree line. Before the tax, if government purchases are $40 billion, the equilibrium level of income is $200 billion. After the tax, income is $125 billion, assuming that government purchases are still $40 billion. Thus, the increase in taxes of $50 billion reduced income by $75 billion.

The equilibrium level of income can also be determined from the following set of equations:

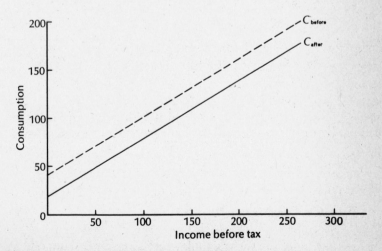

Figure 5-2   Consumption Before and After Taxes

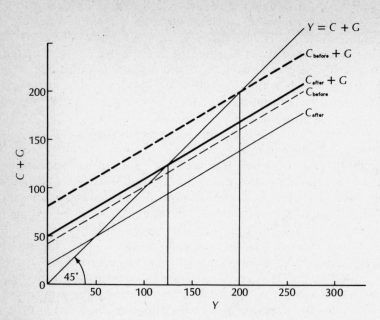

Figure 5-3   Income Before and After Taxes

$$Y = C + G \qquad \text{Social account}$$
$$C = 40 + .6(Y - T) \qquad \text{Consumption function}$$

Government purchases are a constant $40 billion, while taxes are alternatively zero or $50 billion. Where no tax is levied, the solution is

$$Y = 40 + .6(Y - 0) + 40$$
$$.4Y = 80$$
$$Y = 200$$

Where taxes are $50, income equals

$$Y = 40 + .6(Y - 50) + 40$$
$$.4Y = 50$$
$$Y = 125$$

Consumption can be found by substituting income and taxes into the consumption function. In the first case, where no tax is levied,

$$C = 40 + .6(200 - 0)$$
$$= 160$$

In the second case, where taxes are a lump sum of $50 billion,

$$C = 40 + .6(125 - 50)$$
$$= 85$$

Consumption declines by $75 billion $(75 = 160 - 85)$, which is the whole decline in income.

Table 5-2 Equilibrium Before and After a Lump Sum Tax
(billions of constant dollars)

			I PRODUCERS			
			C_{before}	160		
	Y_{before}	200	C_{after}	85		
	Y_{after}	125				
			G_{before}	40		
			G_{after}	40		
II CONSUMERS				III GOVERNMENT		
C_{before} 160			G_{before}	40		
C_{after} 85			G_{after}	40		
					T_{before}	0
T_{before} 0	Y_{before}	200			T_{after}	50
T_{after} 50	after	125	Surplus			
			before	−40		
S_{before} 40			after	10		
S_{after} −10						

The social accounts in Table 5–2 show the equilibrium quantities for all transactions, including personal saving (S) and the government surplus. Before the tax, households save $40 billion, which is used to finance the government deficit. Funds go to the government by way of the financial markets rather than the tax collector. Households could, for example, buy government bonds. After the tax, the government runs a surplus, because taxes ($50 billion) exceed purchases ($40 billion). The $10 billion surplus now finances households, which dissave by that amount. Households could, for example, cash in their bonds. If one sector runs a surplus, another must run a deficit. Thus, the $50-billion tax turns consumers into net borrowers instead of net lenders.

The contraction of income and consumption is a multiple of the tax increase. When the tax is first levied, disposable income is reduced by $50 billion, which by itself would reduce consumption by $30 billion, given a marginal propensity to consume of .6. However, this reduction in consumption causes income to fall, which produces a further reduction in consumption. Since government purchases do not change, the whole decline in income is due to the decline in consumption.

The tax multiplier (k_{tax}) measures the change in income due to a change in tax receipts.

$$k_{tax} = \frac{\text{change in income}}{\text{change in tax receipts}}$$

If a $50-billion tax reduces income by $75 billion, the tax multiplier is −1.5:

$$k_{tax} = \frac{-75}{50}$$
$$= -1.5$$

The tax multiplier is negative and smaller in absolute value than the government purchases multiplier. It is negative, because a tax increase reduces income. It is smaller in absolute value than the government purchases multiplier, because a tax increase does not reduce income directly but only induces a change in consumption. Government purchases are a component of aggregate demand and, therefore, change income directly as well as indirectly through induced consumption. Like the government purchases multiplier (k), the tax multiplier (k_{tax}) depends on the marginal propensity to consume (*MPC*).[1]

$$k_{tax} = \frac{-MPC}{1-MPC}$$

In the previous example the marginal propensity to consume out of disposable income was .6, so that the tax multiplier was

---

[1] The tax multiplier can be derived as follows: First, substitute the consumption function and an autonomous level of government purchases into the social accounting equation,

$$Y = 40 + .6(Y - T) + G$$

where .6 is the marginal propensity to consume (*MPC*). Second, solve for Y,

$$Y = 40 + .6Y - .6T + G$$
$$Y - .6Y = 40 - .6T + G$$
$$Y = \frac{1}{1-.6}(40 - .6T + G)$$

Third, a small change in taxes (ΔT) produces a corresponding change in income (ΔY), so that the new level of income becomes ($Y + \Delta Y$):

$$Y + \Delta Y = \frac{1}{1-.6}[40 - .6(T + \Delta T) + G]$$

Fourth, subtracting the last equation in the second step from the equation in the third step obtains

$$\Delta Y = \frac{-.6}{1-.6}(\Delta T)$$

The tax multiplier (k_{tax}) is simply the change in income (ΔY) divided by the change in taxes (ΔT), or

$$k_{tax} = \frac{\Delta Y}{\Delta T}$$
$$= \frac{-.6}{1-.6}$$
$$= \frac{-MPC}{1-MPC}$$

$$k_{tax} = \frac{-.6}{1-.6}$$
$$= -1.5$$

Income Tax When taxes are a function of income, the determination of income and the multiplier are more complicated. If government purchases are increased, income tends to rise by a multiple; but the rise in income causes tax receipts to rise. As has just been shown, a rise in tax receipts has a negative effect on income. Thus, the multiplier formulas developed earlier have to be modified when taxes vary with income.

A simple income tax can be represented by the following equation:

$$T = .2Y$$

which shows that taxes (T) are 20 percent of income (Y) at every level of income. If income is \$100 billion, taxes are \$20 billion; if income is \$150 billion, tax receipts will be \$30 billion. The tax rate applied to the last dollar of income is called the marginal tax rate (MTR). In this example, the marginal tax rate is 20 percent at all levels of income; an extra \$50 billion in income increases taxes by \$10 billion, or by 20 percent. In practice the marginal tax rate rises as personal income rises.

When taxes are a function of income, the model for the economy becomes the following:

$$Y = C + G \qquad \text{Social account}$$
$$C = 40 + .6(C - T) \qquad \text{Consumption function}$$
$$T = .2Y \qquad \text{Tax function}$$

Assume government purchases (G) are a constant \$40 billion. The model is the same as before, except that it contains one more equation and one more unknown—namely, the tax equation and the amount of taxes. This system of equations can be solved by substitution. For income, first substitute the tax equation into the consumption function; then substitute the consumption equation and government purchases into the social account.

$$Y = 40 + .6[Y - (.2Y)] + 40$$
$$= 80 + .48Y$$
$$.52Y = 80$$
$$Y = 153.8$$

For taxes, given the equilibrium level of income $(Y = 153.8)$,

$$T = .2Y$$
$$= .2(153.8)$$
$$= 30.8$$

For consumption, given the equilibrium levels of income and taxes,

$$C = 40 + .6(153.8 - 30.8)$$
$$= 113.8$$

The fact that $Y = C + G$ in equilibrium can be used as a check ($153.8 = 113.8 + 40$). Since government purchases exceed tax receipts, the government has a deficit (deficit $= G - T$; $9.2 = 40 - 30.8$). Personal saving equals income after consumption and taxes ($S = Y - C - T$; $9.2 = 153.8 - 113.8 - 30.8$); and it also equals the government deficit ($9.2 = 9.2$), which it finances. All of these quantities can be put into a system of social accounts like Table 5–2.

Now, if government purchases are raised by $10 billion to $50 billion, the level of income rises, but not by as much as in the case where taxes are a lump sum that is unaffected by income. Where government purchases are $50 billion, the equilibrium level of income becomes

$$Y = 40 + .6[Y - (.2Y)] + 50$$
$$= 90 + .48Y$$
$$.52Y = 90$$
$$Y = 173.0$$

Since income rises by $19.2 billion ($19.2 = 173.0 - 153.8$) because of a $10-billion increase in government purchases, the government purchases multiplier now equals approximately 1.92 ($1.92 = 19.2 \div 10 =$ change in income $\div$ change in government purchases),[2] instead of 2.5 shown in the earlier chapters. The govern-

---

[2] When the tax equation is substituted into the consumption equation, which in turn is substituted into the social accounting equation, the following obtains:

$$Y = 40 + .6[Y - (.2Y)] + G$$
$$= 40 + .6(1 - .2)Y + G$$
$$= \frac{1}{1 - .6(1 - .2)}(40 + G)$$

where the marginal propensity to consume (MPC) and the marginal tax rate (MTR) are .6 and .2, respectively. Thus, a change in G causes a multiple change in Y of

$$k = \frac{1}{1 - MPC(1 - MTR)}$$
$$= \frac{1}{1 - .6(1 - .2)}$$
$$= 1.92$$

which is smaller than the earlier government purchases multiplier.

ment purchases multiplier is reduced because an increase in government purchases now increases taxes at the same time that it increases income. Since consumers spend what they have left after taxes, the rise in taxes prevents an autonomous change in government purchases from inducing as large an increase in consumption as occurs without an income tax.

The income tax is called an *automatic stabilizer*, because it reduces the size of fluctuations in income and output. During a depression, when income is falling, tax receipts also fall, so that consumption expenditures do not fall as far as they would if disposable income (income after taxes) were reduced by the whole amount of the fall in personal income. During a period of prosperity, when income is rising, consumption is held down by the automatic rise in tax receipts. Thus, the personal income tax tends to stabilize GNP.

Under the present income tax system, where the marginal tax rate rises as the income of households rises, the income tax can retard the growth of output. If the average person earns $5,000 a year when GNP is $100 billion and $10,000 a year when GNP is $200 billion, total tax receipts rise from $20 billion to $40 billion if the marginal tax rate is a constant 20 percent. However, if the marginal tax rate rises from 20 percent to 30 percent as average income rises from $5,000 to $10,000 per household, total tax receipts will rise from $20 billion to $60 billion. This extra increase in tax receipts that occurs as the marginal tax rate drifts upward tends to retard the growth in GNP. It becomes what is sometimes called a *fiscal drag* on the economy. To counteract this drag and to stimulate the growth of the economy, the government should reduce the schedule of marginal tax rates from time to time. Such a tax cut was proposed under the Kennedy administration and carried out under the Johnson administration. It helped prolong the prosperity of the 1960s.

Government Purchases and Taxes

Governments frequently try to balance their budgets. To avoid deficits, they must impose taxes to equal their expenditures. An increase in government purchases produces a multiple expansion in income, but an increase in taxes causes a multiple contraction. The net impact on income is measured by the *balanced budget* multiplier.

Suppose government purchases and tax receipts are both $40 billion and then are both raised to $50 billion. What happens to income? The equations used earlier provide the answer. In the first case, the equilibrium level of income is

$$Y = 40 + .6(Y - 40) + 40$$
$$.4Y = 56$$
$$Y = 140$$

In the second case, where both purchases and taxes are $10 billion more, income is

$$Y = 40 + .6(Y - 50) + 50$$
$$.4Y = 60$$
$$Y = 150$$

Thus, income rises by $10 billion, which is the same as the increase in purchases and taxes. The balanced budget multiplier equals one for this two-sector economy, which ignores investment and foreign trade.

The balanced budget multiplier is equal to one[3] because government purchases increase income by the amount of the purchases plus induced consumption, while the tax increase reduces income by the amount of the induced consumption. The government purchases increase income when they are made, but the taxes prevent disposable income from rising. Consumption remains unchanged, and the only increase in spending is the government purchases.

Fiscal Policy Tools

Unemployment, inflation, and foreign trade are three principal macroeconomic problem areas facing the government. Purchases, taxes, transfers, and deficits are the main fiscal tools available for their solution. At the macroeconomic level, these tools operate through their effect on aggregate demand. In general, the greater the demand for goods and services, the smaller is the amount of unemployment, but the greater is the tendency for prices to rise and for the balance of payments to show a deficit. However, this section is mainly concerned with the effect of fiscal policy on aggregate demand, not the effect of aggregate demand on unemployment, inflation, and the balance of payments, which will be discussed later.

---

[3] The balanced budget multiplier ($k_{balance}$) is the sum of the government purchases multiplier (k) and the tax multiplier (k_{tax}):

$$k_{balance} = k + k_{tax}$$
$$= \frac{1}{1 - MPC} + \frac{-MPC}{1 - MPC}$$
$$= \frac{1 - MPC}{1 - MPC}$$
$$= 1$$

Four different fiscal policy questions are considered in this section. Which has the largest multiplier: deficit spending, tax cutting, or balanced budget spending? How do transfers to households affect aggregate demand? What effect does a tax policy or welfare policy that redistributes income have on aggregate demand? Is fiscal policy as effective for a local government as it is for the national government?

The Largest Multiplier As a general rule, an additional dollar of purchases increases aggregate demand more than an equal reduction in taxes, and deficit spending generates more production than the same spending financed with a balanced budget.

The government purchases multiplier is larger than the tax multiplier, so new purchases of a given amount increase income by more than a tax cut of the same amount. In a period of unemployment the government should prefer public works to tax cuts if both could be implemented in the same amount of time. However, public works take time to plan and construct. A hydroelectric dam or national highway may take years to begin, much less complete, by which time unemployment may no longer be a problem. A tax cut puts income in the hands of consumers almost immediately, though consumers may change their spending behavior and frustrate government policy. The government has to choose between the relative certainty of a public works project and the relative speed of a tax cut.

In the 1930s Keynes argued that government expenditures that are utterly useless in themselves may prove worthwhile because of the multiplier. Even if men were paid to carry dirt by the spoonful up a hill and down again, the volume of useful production would be increased, because those men would spend their pay at the grocery and the bar, providing useful employment to others. It would be better if government purchases were useful; but, if they are not, so far as fiscal policy is concerned, a spoonful of dirt is as good as a trip to the moon, provided it costs enough. Indeed, if unemployment is concentrated in the aerospace industry, a trip to the moon may be the best way to get a spoonful of dirt.

Pre-Keynesian politicians opposed deficit spending for two reasons: They did not want the debt to be a burden on future generations, and they did not want to expand the government's role through public works or other expenditures.

The first reason, the idea that the national debt is a burden on future generations, arose in part from a fallacious view of the government. The government was likened to an individual household with a limited life. Any debts incurred by the head of a household that are not paid off by the time of his death will reduce the inheritance of his heirs. This individualistic view of the government led politicians to oppose deficit spending and to favor balanced budgets, except in time of war. Deficit spending in wartime could be justified on the grounds that war protected the state itself; and, in any event, at such times deficit spending is unavoidable. Today much of the national debt of the major world powers was incurred to finance major wars.

Under certain circumstances, however, the government debt can be a burden on present as well as future generations. For example, if the debt is incurred at a time of full employment, it will tend to cause inflation, which is a burden that most people want to avoid. If the debt is financed by a system of taxation that redistributes income from one group to another, it becomes a burden on part of the population. This occurs in the case of state and local bonds in the United States, because the interest on them is exempt from the federal income tax. The rich buy the bonds to avoid taxes, while the rest of the population pay the taxes that finance the interest charges. Finally, if the debt is ever paid off through higher taxes, it will tend to reduce output and may cause unemployment. Once a large public debt exists, it can be reduced without causing a depression only during a period of extraordinarily high private spending.

Also, many pre-Keynesian politicians wanted to limit the role of the government in society—the second argument against deficit spending. They thought that private spending was of greater benefit to the public than government spending, because each individual knows his personal needs better than the government. However, nearly everyone recognizes that private individuals can not provide for all their needs. Highways, education, sanitation, and many other goods and services have been supplied by the government for a long time. Where the line should be drawn between private and public spending is a political question that economics can not answer. Hopefully, politicians will ask whether government or private spending in a particular area produces the greatest benefit at the least cost. They should also ask how each project affects the political, social, and cultural fabric of society and whether it disturbs the balance of nature.

Transfer Payments Transfer payments from governments to households are transactions that do not involve the exchange of factor services, current production, or IOUs. They include unemployment compensation, old-age benefits, relief, interest on the public debt, and several dozen smaller items. Interest on the public debt is included because it is primarily related to past activity, especially debts incurred to finance major wars; therefore, government interest payments are not made in exchange for the use of capital resources to produce current output.

Transfer payments cause a multiple expansion of income and output. While they do not increase aggregate demand directly, they increase the disposable income of households and induce households to increase consumption, as tax cuts do. The transfer payments multiplier ($k_{transfers}$) is the same absolute magnitude as the tax multiplier, but it is positive in sign.

$$k_{transfers} = \frac{MPC}{1 - MPC}$$

If taxes are raised to finance transfers, aggregate demand will not be affected, except (perhaps) through a redistribution of income.

Unemployment compensation can be used to check unemployment. Payments to the unemployed can prevent a decline in autonomous spending from developing into a serious depression. By maintaining the level of disposable income, unemployment compensation tends to maintain consumption and, thereby, employment. Since unemployment payments rise automatically as unemployment rises, they are called an automatic stabilizer. They rise during depression and fall during prosperity. The income tax is an automatic stabilizer for the same reason. Automatic stabilizers do not prevent income from changing, but they retard its progress either up or down.

Income Redistribution Fiscal policy can redistribute income from the rich to the poor. A tax that requires the rich to pay a larger percentage of their income in taxes than the poor is called a *progressive* tax. The income tax is an example of a progressive tax for the typical wage or salary earner; the tax rate rises with income. Investment and business income is subject to a number of exemptions, deductions, and special rates that tend to counteract the progressive nature of the income tax rate structure. The tax exemption of interest on state and local bonds is an example. A *proportional* tax requires all income classes to pay the same percentage of their income in taxes, while a *regressive* tax collects a larger percentage of the income from a poor man than a rich man. A sales tax on an inferior good like bread is regressive. Old-age benefits, unemployment compensation, and relief payments are transfers that tend to redistribute income from the rich to the poor.

The redistribution of income from the rich to the poor will tend to increase production if the rich have a smaller marginal propensity to consume than the poor, that is, if the consumption curve rises at a declining rate. Under these circumstances, a redistribution of income raises the marginal propensity to consume for the whole nation, which increases the equilibrium level of income. For example, given the following government purchases multiplier,

$$k = \frac{1}{1 - MPC}$$

if *MPC* is .6, the multiplier is 2.5; but if the *MPC* is .7, the multiplier is 3.33. Thus, for any amount of government purchases, the equilibrium level of income will be higher, the higher the *MPC*.

The effect of income redistribution from the rich to the poor depends on the initial distribution of income as well as the marginal propensity to consume of the two groups. If a few people receive a large proportion of the national income, the poor can receive a large increase in their income with redistribution and can increase their consumption substantially. The more equal the distribution of income to begin with, the smaller will be the effect of redistribution on aggregate demand.

Fiscal Policy and Local Government   Local governments can not combat unemployment or inflation with fiscal policy as readily as can national governments, though they have occasionally undertaken public works projects to absorb part of the unemployed and have regulated rents to control part of inflation. Government purchases, tax cuts, and transfer payments made in one city increase the demand for goods and services in that city; but, while the final purchases are made in that city, the goods are often made elsewhere. A city has an *open economy*: a large portion of its transactions are with people and enterprises outside the city. Inflation and unemployment are often caused by what happens to aggregate demand in the national economy. Nation states confront the same problem to a lesser extent because of foreign trade; their economies are open to the forces at work in world markets.

FOREIGN
TRADE

Foreign trade affects the volume of output, the amount of employment, and the level of prices in each country that makes international transactions; and each country affects world markets to the extent of its foreign trade. The balance of payments has a significant influence on the domestic economy and on macroeconomic policy, though before the dramatic world monetary crises of August 1971 and February 1973 the importance of the balance of payments was occasionally overlooked. This chapter presents the theoretical relationships between foreign trade and the domestic economy, while Chapter 10 is concerned with balance-of-payments policy.

The balance of payments account that was presented earlier, Table 2–9, summarizes the transactions that occur between one country and the rest of the world. Current transactions include goods and services plus transfer payments; capital flows involve either long-term or short-term financial transactions. The change in official reserves appears as a use of funds, and under a system of fixed exchange rates it balances the account when a surplus or deficit occurs through capital account. For example, in Table 2–9 a deficit existed through current and capital accounts, so that the country had to draw down its holdings of official reserves. A surplus increases official reserves. But what determines the volume of current and capital transactions? Why should a surplus or deficit arise?

The balance of exports and imports is explained by the reciprocal demands for goods and services that enter international trade. In Chapter 1 the demand for products was shown to depend on income and prices. For a typical product, the quantity demanded rises as income rises and also rises as its price falls relative to other prices. These two factors are considered one at a time in separate sections. Transfers are left to one side for the moment. Capital transactions are influenced by the rates of return and the rates of interest in one country relative to another, which is discussed in another section. The final section of this chapter explains the relation of the foreign exchange rate to the balance of payments.

Income and Trade

Net exports (exports minus imports) is the fourth component of aggregate demand. As a component of aggregate demand, it helps determine income; but, in addition, income affects net exports, because the demand for imports depends on the level of domestic income—an increase in income increases imports. Therefore, given a constant level of exports, net exports tend to fall as income rises. This complicates the problem of income determination.

The import schedule, Table 6–1, shows that imports rise as income rises. Both imports and income are measured in constant dollars per year. A constant dollar measurement eliminates price changes so that the quantity of goods and services imported (or exported) can be isolated and analyzed. Where income is $50 billion, imports are $5 billion; where income is $100 billion, imports are $10 billion. The increase in imports due to an increase in income is measured by the *marginal propensity to import (MPM)*.

Table 6-1   The Import Schedule

INCOME Y (billions of constant dollars)	IMPORTS M	MARGINAL PROPENSITY TO IMPORT MPM
0	0	
		.1
50	5	
		.1
100	10	
		.1
150	15	
		.1
200	20	
		.1
250	25	

$$MPM = \frac{\text{change in imports}}{\text{change in income}}$$

Since imports rise by \$5 billion in Table 6–1 for every \$50-billion rise in income, the marginal propensity to import is .1 at every level of income ($5 \div 50 = .1$).

The import curve in Figure 6–1 is graphed from the data in Table 6–1. This import curve is an Engel curve that is positively sloped, indicating that imports are ordinary goods—a greater quantity is demanded at higher levels of income. In this example, no imports are demanded at a zero level of income; thus, the import curve passes through the origin of the graph, that is, the intercept is zero. Each extra dollar of income increases the quantity of imports demanded by one-tenth of a dollar. The

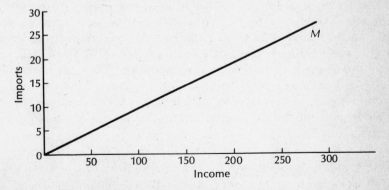

Figure 6-1   Import Function

marginal propensity to import is, therefore, the slope of the import curve. Since the intercept is zero and the marginal propensity to import is .1, the equation for the import curve is the following:

$$M = .1\,Y$$

where M stands for imports and Y stands for income. If income is $100 billion, imports are $10 billion ($10 = .1 \times 100$); and if income is $200 billion, imports are $20 billion ($20 = .1 \times 200$).

The equilibrium level of income and imports for a simplified economy is illustrated in Table 6–2. The economy is

Table 6-2   Equilibrium with Foreign Trade (billions of constant dollars)

INCOME Y	CONSUMPTION C	EXPORTS X	IMPORTS M	AGGREGATE DEMAND C+X−M
0	40	10	0	50
50	70	10	5	75
100	100	10	10	**100**
150	130	10	15	125
200	160	10	20	150
250	190	10	25	175

simplified by ignoring investment and government purchases, so that consumption and net exports are the only components of aggregate demand. The first two columns present the same consumption function that was discussed in Chapter 3: consumption rises less than in proportion to an increase in income. Exports are assumed to be a constant $10 billion at every level of domestic income. No doubt foreign income affects exports, but this carries the analysis beyond a single country. The relation between imports and income is the same as in Table 6–1. The last column computes aggregate demand—consumption plus exports minus imports—at every level of income. Equilibrium exists where aggregate demand equals income, which occurs at $100 billion. At an income of $100 billion, consumption plus exports minus imports equals income.

The relationships in Table 6–2 can be shown by a set of simultaneous equations, the solution to which is equilibrium.

$$Y = C + X - M \qquad \text{Social account}$$
$$C = 40 + .6Y \qquad \text{Consumption function}$$
$$M = .1Y \qquad \text{Import function}$$
$$X = 10 \qquad \text{Exports defined}$$

The first equation is the simplified social account for producers (government purchases and investment are assumed to equal zero); the second equation is the consumption function; the third is the import function; and the last defines the level of exports. The equilibrium level of income is obtained by substituting the last three equations into the first:

$$Y = 40 + .6Y + 10 - .1Y$$
$$= 50 + .5Y$$
$$.5Y = 50$$
$$Y = 100$$

Where income is $100 billion, consumption is $100 billion and imports are $10 billion. In this particular example, imports equal exports; the international payments account shows neither a surplus nor a deficit for goods and services.

An increase in exports, which can be thought of as an autonomous expenditure, increases income by a multiple. The foreign trade multiplier (k_{trade}) shows the change in income associated with a one-dollar change in exports (autonomous spending):

$$k_{trade} = \frac{\text{change in income}}{\text{change in exports}}$$

This foreign trade multiplier is not as large as the autonomous expenditures multiplier discussed in Chapter 3, because a portion of the change in income is spent abroad. An increase in exports produces a change in income, which induces consumers to spend more. However, as income rises, more goods are imported, so that total domestic spending does not increase by as much as it would if imports were constant. If exports rise to $20 billion, the equilibrium level of income is

$$Y = 40 + .6Y + 20 - .1Y$$
$$.5Y = 60$$
$$Y = 120$$

Since income rises by $20 billion as exports rise by $10 billion, the foreign trade multiplier is 2.0.[1]

$$k_{trade} = \frac{20}{10}$$
$$= 2.0$$

If imports had not increased (that is, if $MPM=0$), the multiplier would have been 2.5, as discussed in Chapter 3.

The marginal propensity to import explains why government fiscal policies that are intended to eliminate unemployment are less effective in small countries that depend heavily on foreign trade than they are in large countries that are more self-sufficient. For example, fiscal policy in Canada is probably less effective than fiscal policy in the United States, because Canada imports a larger portion of the goods it uses than does the United States. The higher the marginal propensity to import, the smaller is the government purchases multiplier and the smaller is the effect of public spending on employment. A city government that tried to reduce unemployment with a public works project might find that its multiplier was less than one if a large part of the materials and services used in the project originated outside of the city.

The level of prosperity in each country is tied to the world economy by the effect of income on imports and exports. If a major depression occurs in Europe, Europe will import less from North America, which will export less and will suffer a mul-

---

[1] The foreign trade multiplier can be calculated in the following manner. First, substitute the consumption function, exports, and the import function into the income account and solve for income:

$$Y = 40 + .6Y + X - .1Y$$
$$Y - .6Y + .1Y = 40 + X$$

$$Y = \frac{1}{1 - .6 + .1}(40 + X)$$

Second, the foreign trade multiplier (k_{trade}) is the change in income (ΔY) divided by the change in exports (ΔX) or some other autonomous expenditure:

$$k_{trade} = \frac{\Delta Y}{\Delta X}$$

$$= \frac{1}{1 - .6 + .1}$$

$$= 2.00$$

$$= \frac{1}{1 - MPC + MPM}$$

where MPC is the marginal propensity to consume and MPM is the marginal propensity to import.

tiple contraction in production. As income in North America declines, North America will import less from Europe, creating a vicious circle. During the Great Depression of the 1930s, many countries tried to isolate themselves from the rest of the world by erecting barriers to imports. They thought that net exports and employment could be maintained. Unfortunately, this was a game that any number could play. One country can always retaliate against the restrictive trade policies of other countries. As a result, the total volume of world trade in the 1930s was greatly reduced by restrictive policies, which proved to be worse than the problem they were intended to solve.

Prices and Trade

The demand for imports and for exports follows the law of demand—the higher the price, the smaller the quantity demanded. This is illustrated in Figure 6–2, which shows that the demand curves for both imports and exports are negatively sloped. For exports, the relevant price is the price of goods produced domestically relative to the price of the same goods produced abroad, given the exchange rate. If the domestic price rises relative to the world price (P_1 to P_2), the quantity of exports demanded falls (Q_1 to Q_2). The price ratio is reversed for imports. A rise in domestic prices relative to world prices makes foreign goods relatively cheaper to the importer, so a larger quantity is demanded.

Goods and services in the balance of payments account are measured by the dollar value of imports and exports. The dollar value of a transaction equals the price times the quantity sold. When prices are constant, as was assumed in the previous section, changes in the constant dollar value of imports or exports reflect only changes in the quantities exchanged. However, when prices change, as in Figure 6–2, the dollar value of

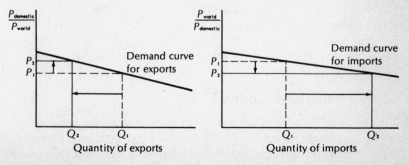

Figure 6-2   Demand Curves for Exports and Imports

imports and exports changes because both prices and quantities changed. Because of the law of demand, price and quantity change in opposite directions; if price declines, quantity rises. What happens to price times quantity? What happens to the dollar value of exports minus imports?

If the quantity demanded rises by a larger percentage than the fall in price, the dollar value of exports (or imports) rises. The increase in the quantity sold more than compensates for the fact that every unit is sold at a lower price; the demand curve is said to be *elastic*, as explained in Chapter 1. Demand curves need not be elastic; but in the case of imports and exports, it is realistic to assume that they are elastic. Each country is in competition with many other countries for world markets. A price decline in the goods sold by one country will affect the quantity demanded substantially. For example, Canada and the United States are both major wheat exporters. If one sells at a slightly lower price than the other, it will be able to sell a much larger volume than the other, because it is in the self-interest of the importer to buy as cheaply as possible. Thus, the export demand for wheat of each country is elastic. The same can be said of most products entering international trade.

During a period of inflation in the home country, when the average level of product prices is rising, the balance of payments is affected. Export prices rise relative to world prices, and import prices fall relative to domestic prices, assuming the exchange rate is fixed. If the demand curves for exports and imports are elastic, the dollar value of exports falls and the dollar value of imports rises, because the percentage change in the quantities demanded exceeds the percentage change in prices. Therefore, net exports decline, and the country tends to run a deficit in its balance of payments for goods and services. In terms of Figure 6–2, if domestic prices rise relative to world prices, both the quantity and dollar value of exports decline. The dollar value of exports can be viewed as the rectangles (sales equal price times quantity) inscribed by the demand curve; similarly for imports. At the same time, domestic inflation increases the quantity and dollar value of imports as foreign goods become relatively cheaper. Net exports decline. Inflation is a problem for governments partly because of its effect on the balance of payments.

Interest Rates and Capital Flows

The balance-of-payments capital account records international financial transactions. A capital transaction is classified as short-term if the financial claim comes due within a year, such as a 90-day loan from a bank; otherwise it is classified as a long-term transaction. The direct acquisition by a foreigner of a domestic capital good, such as a factory, is called direct foreign investment and is treated as a long-term capital flow. Long-term capital flows also involve the purchase or sale of securities, such as stocks and bonds. This classification system is used because short-term and long-term capital flows behave differently.

Direct foreign investment depends on the rate of return that an investor can expect on a new or existing capital good. It can be viewed in much the same way as the demand for newly produced capital goods, which was discussed in Chapter 4. The principle of opportunity cost leads an investor to compare one alternative with another. If he expects a higher rate of return on a foreign capital good than on a domestic capital good, his self-interest directs his investment abroad.

The rate of return in a foreign country may exceed what can be earned at home for several reasons. First, more capital is accumulated in the developed countries of the world than in the newly emerging nations, so that the marginal product of capital may be greater in a less developed than in a more developed country. This tends to attract capital to the less developed countries. Second, richer deposits of natural resources may be located abroad than at home. For example, the oil fields in Europe and the United States are not sufficient for domestic consumption. More productive fields, which yield higher rates of return, exist in the Middle East and Africa. Therefore, the international oil companies go where the profits are greatest, instead of investing capital in high-cost fields at home. Third, trade barriers may make foreign investment more profitable than domestic investment. If a country taxes imports heavily, a foreign company may find that it is more profitable to acquire a factory in that country than it is to build a factory at home and export to that country.

In financial markets, transactors try to earn the highest rate of return on their financial assets and pay the lowest rate of interest on their liabilities, given the risk, liquidity, and other terms of financial contracts. For example, if interest rates are higher in Canada than in the United States, an international corporation will prefer to borrow in the United States, if it can, and keep its financial assets in Canada, if it has an excess of funds above its immediate business needs. This would produce a net outflow of funds from the United States to Canada. In general, the higher the rate of interest in one country relative to the rest of the world, the greater is the inflow of funds on capital account, both long-term and short-term. Short-term funds that move quickly from country to country in response to interest rate differentials or in response to exchange rates are sometimes called *hot money*.

Capital flows are also directly related to imports and exports, especially in the case of short-term capital flows. Short-term capital flows are often viewed as accommodating transactions that finance more basic trade or long-term capital movements. Not only are particular import and export transactions financed on credit, but a general surplus or deficit on trade account is often financed on credit. An excess of imports over exports can be offset by a net inflow of short-term funds. If private individuals and financial institutions do not finance a deficit, the government may push up interest rates in order to attract funds. Otherwise its official reserves will be drawn down, which may force it to change its exchange rate.

The Exchange Rate

An exchange rate is the price of one currency in terms of another currency. Each country has its own currency, which is legal tender only within the boundaries of that country. A traveler from one country to another finds that he must change his money into the national currency of each country he enters. The ratio in which the currencies are traded is called the exchange rate. If $2.50 in U.S. currency buys one British pound, the price of the pound in terms of dollars is $2.50. There was a day when the pound cost $5.00, but the pound has fallen in value, or *depreciated*, since that time. If a currency rises in value, it is said to *appreciate*. As the British pound depreciated from $5.00 to $2.50 over the years, the U.S. dollar appreciated. At first the dollar cost £.20, but recently it cost £.40, which means it now takes more British currency to buy a U.S. dollar.

A system of fixed exchange rates exists when governments agree to maintain official rates of exchange between currencies or between currencies and gold. The term *devalue* is used when the value of a currency is reduced officially, historically in terms of gold. The U.S. dollar has recently been devalued twice in terms of gold: first, from $35 to $38 per ounce; second, from $38 to $42.22 per ounce of gold. *Revalue* refers to an official appreciation.

A system of flexible exchange rates exists when the supply and demand for each currency determines its value. Canada, among other countries, has let its dollar float from time to time in order to establish its market value. Where exchange rates are flexible, the market mechanism tends to keep the balance of payments in equilibrium.

Figure 6–3 illustrates how the market mechanism affects the exchange rate. The dollar is assumed to be the domestic

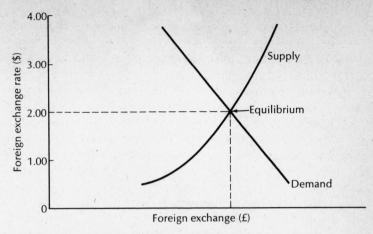

Figure 6-3   Demand and Supply for Foreign Exchange

currency and the pound is the foreign currency. The exchange rate on the vertical axis measures the price of the pound in terms of dollars, that is, in dollars per pound. When two dollars buy one pound, the price of the pound is $2.00; when dollars and pounds trade one-for-one, the price of the pound is $1.00. The pound depreciates if its price falls from $2.00 to $1.00; the dollar appreciates at the same time. The quantity of foreign exchange is measured in pounds along the horizontal axis.

The demand for pounds arises from imports of British products and capital outflows to Britain. Imports are ultimately purchased in pounds, and capital flows to Britain are converted into pounds. The demand curve is downward sloping because a greater quantity of British goods and services are demanded as they become cheaper for Americans to buy. If a British sports car costs £1,000 in the United Kingdom, it costs $2,000 in the United States when the exchange rate is $2.00 per pound (ignoring transportation costs); but it costs only $1,000 in the United States if the pound depreciates to $1.00. The quantity of pounds demanded in order to buy British products increases as the pound depreciates, that is, as the dollar appreciates.

The supply curve reflects the use of pounds by people in Britain to buy American exports and send capital to the United States. It slopes upward if the demand for exports is elastic. American exports become more expensive for the British to buy as the pound depreciates (dollar appreciates), so that a smaller quantity is demanded. If the demand curve for American exports is elastic, not only is a smaller quantity of exports demanded as the pound depreciates, but a smaller total amount is spent as well. For example, if a truck costs $6,000 in the United States, it would sell for £3,000 in Britain (ignoring transportation costs) when the exchange rate is $2.00 per pound. If the pound depreciated to $1.00 per pound, the American truck would cost £6,000 in the United Kingdom. Thus, a smaller quantity of American trucks would be demanded at the $1.00 per pound exchange rate than at the $2.00 per pound rate. When the demand curve for exports is elastic, a smaller amount in total is spent on exports as they become more expensive or, what amounts to the same thing, as the pound becomes less valuable. The quantity of pounds supplied to buy American exports decreases as the pound depreciates.

The balance of payments is in equilibrium where the quantity of pounds supplied equals the quantity demanded. In Figure 6–3, equilibrium occurs at $2.00 per pound. If the value of the pound were below equilibrium, American goods would be more expensive and British goods would be cheaper than at the equilibrium exchange rate. For example, at an exchange rate of $1.00 per pound, a £1,000 British car costs only $1,000 in the United States, whereas it costs $2,000 at a $2.00 per pound exchange rate. Thus, imports into the United States would be greater at $1.00 than at $2.00 per pound. Similarly, if an American truck sells for $6,000 in the United States, it would cost £6,000 in Britain at $1.00 per pound but only £3,000 at $2.00 per pound. Thus, below the equilibrium exchange rate of $2.00 per pound, the quantity of pounds demanded exceeds the quantity of pounds supplied, and the tendency is for the value of the pound to rise as Americans outbid one another for the limited quantity of pounds available in order to buy British goods. As the value of the pound rises, American spending on imports falls and foreign spending on exports rises until equilibrium is established. Above the equilibrium exchange rate, market forces tend to push the exchange rate down to the equilibrium level.

In order to maintain a fixed exchange rate, the government must enter the market to counteract the forces that are pushing the exchange rate up or down. This is why a country has international reserves. If its exchange rate is falling, it buys its own currency on the world market with its reserves, which tends to raise the value of its own currency; and if its exchange rate rises above the official rate, it sells its currency in exchange for gold or other reserves, which tends to depress the value of its currency.

At Bretton Woods in 1944 the major non-Communist countries agreed to fix their exchange rates in terms of the U.S. dollar, the British pound, or gold. The International Monetary

Fund (IMF) was established to supervise this system. Each country was expected to maintain the value of its currency, at least within a narrow range of prices, at an official rate of exchange. If a country ran a balance-of-payments surplus, its central bank was supposed to buy foreign currencies or gold in order to hold down the value of its own currency to the official exchange rate. It bought foreign currency or gold, which accumulated as official reserves, with its own currency. The purchase of foreign exchange shifted the demand curve out in Figure 6–3 and tended to stop the value of foreign currencies from depreciating (domestic currency from appreciating). If a country ran a balance-of-payments deficit, its central bank was supposed to buy its own currency with its official reserves. This shifted the supply of foreign exchange out and tended to keep the foreign exchange rate from rising (domestic currency from falling). In terms of Figure 6–3, balance-of-payments surpluses occur at exchange rates above the equilibrium point and deficits occur below the equilibrium point.

The official reserves of each country and of the world are limited, so that a large and persistent balance-of-payments disequilibrium must ultimately be corrected or the official exchange rate changed. Under the Bretton Woods system, if a country ran a deficit, the IMF would at first insist that the cause of the deficit be eliminated. A minor deficit could be corrected by restricting domestic income, which would reduce the demand for imports and tend to depress domestic prices relative to prices in the rest of the world, or by increasing interest rates, which would tend to attract foreign funds. In the meantime, the IMF might lend the country funds to augment its official reserves. If the deficit proved to be a "fundamental disequilibrium" that could not be easily corrected, the IMF would approve an exchange rate depreciation.

A world monetary crisis occurred in 1971 when it became apparent that the United States had a fundamental balance-of-payments disequilibrium that could not be corrected. The official reserves of the United States were held in gold, which other countries were demanding in exchange for their excess dollars. As its gold stock declined, the United States restricted the privilege of redeeming U.S. dollars in gold to major central banks and discouraged those central banks from using that privilege. However, the deficit continued. Finally, in August 1971, the dollar was declared to be inconvertible; no more dollars would be accepted in exchange for gold. The United States government devalued the dollar in terms of gold, though only after the market had depreciated it in terms of foreign currencies, on the assumption that exports would rise and imports would fall until the United States balance of payments was in equilibrium. However, a second devaluation became necessary in February 1973.

The Bretton Woods agreement collapsed when the U.S. dollar depreciated in 1971. It was followed by the short-lived Smithsonian agreement, which ended with the depreciation of the U.S. dollar in February 1973. Subsequent negotiations have failed to produce a general agreement, though they have established a period of cautious anarchy in which exchange rates are neither fixed nor floating in the pure sense. Each country uses its reserves to maintain the value of its currency at what it thinks is a proper level in the face of short-term disruptions, but it lets its currency float as long-term changes occur. The problem of foreign exchange rate policy is left until Chapter 10.

MONEY AND INTEREST

Functions of Money

Money developed because of the difficulty of bartering one good for another. In a barter economy, a double coincidence must be satisfied for each transaction: each transactor must exchange the goods and services that he produces directly for the products that he consumes. An egg farmer who wants to buy potatoes must find a potato farmer who wants to buy eggs. Wherever labor is extensively divided and specialized, exchange by barter is inefficient and impractical. In a money economy, the egg farmer sells his eggs for money, with which he can buy potatoes. The potato farmer sells his potatoes for money, which he can hold for future use if he does not need goods immediately.

Money functions as a medium of exchange, a store of value, and a standard of value. First, goods, services, and IOUs are exchanged for money, the *medium of exchange*. As a medium of exchange, money circulates from hand to hand. Output is sold in the product market in exchange for money, which is distributed to the owners of the factors of production in exchange for their services. Second, the surplus funds that households save can be held as money, *the store of value*, though surplus funds can be stored in other ways. They can be used to buy government bonds or to pay off mortgages; that is, surplus funds can be used to acquire claims on others or settle claims against oneself. Money is a sort of universal claim that everyone accepts; it is the most convenient and most liquid store of value. Third, prices are quoted and accounts are kept in terms of money. As a *standard of value*, money measures the value of all other commodities.

The medium of exchange function is the principal function of money; it provides the traditional definition of money, because it is the only function that money alone performs. Any durable good or financial claim can serve as a store of value, and there are other standards of value besides money. In Britain prices are sometimes quoted in terms of the Guinea, a standard value based on a coin no longer in circulation. Only money serves as a medium of exchange, but what serves as money varies from one time and place to another. Currency in circulation and demand deposits in banks are clearly money, because they are commonly used to transact business. Interest-bearing savings accounts are not a medium of exchange in the United States, but they are in Canada, where checks are written on them. Financial claims that can be converted into money quickly (such as noncheckable savings accounts, savings bonds, and Treasury bills) are called *near-money*. They are nearly as liquid as money, but they are not generally accepted on demand.

Liquidity Preference Theory of Interest

The liquidity preference theory was developed by J. M. Keynes to explain the determination of the rate of interest.[1] For classical economists the rate of interest equates the supply of savings with the demand for capital. For Keynes saving de-

---

[1] J. M. Keynes, *The General Theory of Employment, Interest, and Money* (London: Macmillan, 1936).

pended on income, as discussed in Chapter 3; the rate of interest depends on whether households prefer to hold their accumulated savings in the form of money or bonds. For simplicity Keynes assumed that there was only a single rate of interest and only two types of financial claims—money and bonds.

The liquidity preference theory is expressed in terms of the demand for money, because that part of financial wealth which is not held in the form of money is by assumption held in the form of bonds. Given the amount of financial wealth in the economy, once the demand for money is determined, so is the demand for bonds. According to Keynes, households have three motives for holding money: a transactions motive, a precautionary motive, and a speculative motive.

The *transactions motive* arises from the use of money as a medium of exchange. Income is received at one point in time and purchases are made at other points in time. Money is demanded to cover the time gap between the receipt and expenditure of funds. The greater the volume of transactions and the greater the time gap between income and outlay, the greater is the transactions demand for money. The frequency with which payments are made is mainly determined by custom and does not change rapidly; therefore, the transactions demand for money depends primarily on income and increases as income increases.

The *precautionary motive* arises from imperfect knowledge of the future. The prudent household will hold more cash than it needs for its planned expenditures, because unforeseen events may disrupt its plans. Prices may change, the car may break down, an appliance may need repairs, any number of unexpected expenditures may become necessary. As a rule, the greater the income and consumption of the household, the greater is its demand for precautionary cash balances.

The *speculative motive* arises from the store of value function of money. Funds can be held in the form of idle cash balances, which bear no interest, or in the form of bonds, which earn interest. A household might prefer to forego the interest on a bond if it expected the price of bonds to fall, that is, if it expected that it would not be able to sell the bond for as much as its purchase price. Thus, a household is really speculating on the price of bonds when it holds money in excess of its needs for transactions and precaution.

The relation between the price of a bond and the market rate of interest can be illustrated by the case of a perpetual debenture such as the British Consol. Unlike other bonds, a perpetual debenture never comes due; it has no maturity date at which it must be redeemed. Like most other bonds, it bears a fixed annual interest payment, and it can be bought and sold in a market. Each year its owner is entitled to receive a fixed sum of money called an annuity. Selling the bond transfers title to the annuity to the buyer. If the owner of a perpetual debenture is entitled to receive $50 a year, the bond is worth $1,000 when the market rate of interest is 5 percent (5 percent of $1,000 is $50). As long as the market rate of interest is 5 percent, no one would pay more than $1,000 for the bond, because he would receive less than 5 percent on his money, and no one would sell for less than the market price. However, if the market rate of interest rose to 10 percent, the price of the bond would fall to $500—a $50 annuity is 10 percent of $500. No one would pay more than $500, because everyone wants the highest rate of return he can get. Whoever owned the bond when the market rate of interest rose from 5 percent to 10 percent would suffer a $500-loss in the value of his capital.[2]

Other types of bonds also pay a fixed dollar amount of interest each year, and their prices fluctuate in the market. When the price of bonds falls in the market, the market rate of interest rises. The price of bonds and the rate of interest move inversely. Since the speculative demand for money depends on the price of bonds, it also depends on the rate of interest.

At any point in time, households tend to regard a particular rate of interest as the normal or conventional rate, though opinions about the conventional rate usually differ. Most households expect that any deviation from the normal will be

---

[2] The price of a bond is simply the discounted present value of the stream of income its owner expects to receive. Discounting was discussed in Chapter 4. In the case of a perpetual debenture, the price of the bond (P) is equal to the stream of annuities (A) discounted at the market rate of interest (i):

$$P = \frac{A}{1+i} + \frac{A}{(1+i)^2} + \frac{A}{(1+i)^3} + \cdots$$

It equals the sum of an infinite series, which simplifies to

$$P = \frac{A}{i}$$

Where A is $50 and i is 5 percent (.05), P is $1,000, which is quickly calculated. In the case of bonds that have a maturity date, the owner cashes in the bond when it comes due. He receives a redemption value (R) in addition to an annuity in the last (n^{th}) year of the bond's life. Thus, the present value of the bond is

$$P = \frac{A}{1+i} + \frac{A}{(1+i)^2} + \cdots + \frac{A+R}{(1+i)^n}$$

which can not always be quickly calculated. Still, the price of the bond and the market rate of interest are inversely related.

temporary and that the interest rate will soon move back to its conventional level. If the rate of interest rises, those consumers who expect the rate of interest to fall again will decrease their demand for idle cash balances, because they expect the price of bonds to rise. They will shift their funds from money to bonds in order to benefit from the expected rise in the price of bonds. If the interest rate falls, to give the opposite case, the price of bonds will have risen; and consumers who expect a capital loss from holding bonds will shift their funds out of bonds into money. Thus, the demand for idle cash balances and the rate of interest are inversely related.

The liquidity preference theory is illustrated in Figure 7–1. Since both the transactions and the precautionary demands for money are directly related to the level of income, they are added together under the heading of active cash balances. The graph on the left shows that the demand for active cash balances increases as income increases. It is an Engel curve, which shows that money is an ordinary good. Given the level of income (Y_0), the subjective preferences of consumers as shaped by custom set their demand for active cash balances (M_0). The total money stock is divided between active cash balances and idle cash balances, idle cash balances being held for speculation. That part of the money stock which is not active is idle. The graph on the right shows the demand for active cash balances as a constant (M_0), which has already been determined by the level of income, plus the demand for idle cash balances as a function of the rate of interest. The demand for idle cash balances follows the law of demand: the higher the rate of interest, the smaller the quantity of idle balances demanded; the lower the rate of interest, the greater the quantity of speculative balances demanded.

The money supply is controlled by the central bank in a manner that is discussed in the next sections. In Figure 7–1, where the money supply equals M_1, the rate of interest equals i_1. At that rate of interest the demand for active cash balances plus the demand for idle cash balances equals the supply of money. If the money supply were increased to M_2, an excess supply of money would exist at the first rate of interest. At the first rate of interest, consumers are holding more idle cash balances than they desire. Therefore, they will increase their demand for bonds, which will increase the price of bonds. As the price of bonds rises, the rate of interest will fall until it reaches the new equilibrium rate of interest (i_2).

The money supply may increase so far that no further reduction in the interest rate will occur. The demand curve for idle cash balances may become horizontal and enter what is

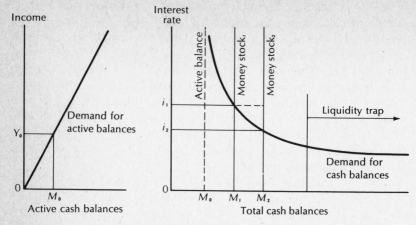

Figure 7-1   The Liquidity Preference Theory

called the *liquidity trap*. The liquidity trap occurs when the rate of interest has fallen so low and, therefore, when the price of bonds has risen so high that everyone expects the price of bonds to fall. No one will increase the demand for bonds further, and everyone will let additional cash balances sit idle rather than risk a loss in the bond market. Keynesians argued that the liquidity trap prevented central banks from reducing interest rates far enough during the Great Depression.

Fractional Reserve Banking

Banks are financial intermediaries. They acquire funds from the public in the form of deposits and advance funds to the public in the form of loans and securities. Most of their profit comes from the difference between the rate of interest paid on deposits and the rate of interest charged on loans and earned on securities. Since the public can withdraw funds on demand from their checking accounts, banks have been required by law to set aside reserves to meet these demands. They are required to keep only a fraction of their deposits on reserve, however, because only a small proportion of their deposits are ever withdrawn by the public at any one time. When one depositor writes a check on a bank, another customer is usually depositing funds with that bank. The net change in reserves is typically a fraction of the total amount of funds on deposit.

The operations of the fractional reserve banking system are reflected in Table 7–1, which is a balance sheet for a commercial bank. Deposits are the principal liability of the bank.

Table 7-1   Balance Sheet for a Commercial Bank, December 31, 1973
(millions of dollars)

ASSETS		LIABILITIES AND NET WORTH		
Reserves	70	Deposits:		
Loans and securities	710	Demand	450	
Buildings and other assets	20	Savings	250	700
		Other liabilities		10
		Net worth		90
Total assets	800	Total claims on assets		800

Demand deposits, as the name indicates, can be withdrawn on demand when a customer writes a check on them. The bank may require notice before savings accounts can be withdrawn, though ordinarily notice is not required. The other liabilities of the bank include funds that it borrows from the public, from other banks, and from the central bank, as well as such minor items as wages and taxes due. Net worth is the residual claim of the bank owners on the assets of the bank. Loans made to customers and securities (mainly government bills, notes, and bonds) purchased in the market are the principal assets and the principal source of revenue for the bank. Buildings and other assets such as furniture and equipment are a small part of total assets. Reserves include both currency (notes and coin) in the bank vault and funds on deposit with the central bank. The law requires the bank to keep a given percentage of its deposits in reserves. Since these reserves do not earn interest for the bank, the profit motive prompts the bank to keep its reserves as close to the legal limit as possible. In Table 7–1, a 10 percent reserve requirement is assumed; reserves of $70 million are 10 percent of the $700 million on deposit. Excess reserves exist when total reserves exceed required reserves.

Table 7–2 is a balance sheet for a central bank, such as the Federal Reserve Bank, the Bank of Canada, or the Bank of

Table 7-2   Balance Sheet for a Central Bank, December 31, 1973
(millions of dollars)

ASSETS		LIABILITIES AND NET WORTH	
Government securities	110,000	Bank notes	50,000
Loans to banks	5,000	Bank reserves	60,000
Buildings and other assets	5,000	Other liabilities	5,000
		Net worth	5,000
Total assets	120,000	Total claims on assets	120,000

England. A central bank performs a variety of functions. It is a *bank of issue*: it has printed and has issued paper bank notes, such as dollar bills, which circulate from hand to hand among the public. These bank notes are a liability of the central bank. It is a *reserve bank*: it holds a part of the reserves of commercial banks on deposit as a liability. These reserves are used to settle accounts between private banks when a check is written on one and deposited in another. It is a *lender of last resort*: a commercial bank can borrow funds from the central bank in order to rebuild its reserves or in order to make additional loans to the public. The central bank also acts on behalf of the government in the government bonds market, in the foreign exchange market, and in the capacity of an ordinary bank. Most important of all, the central bank conducts the monetary policy of the country by controlling the volume of money and credit.

The total stock of money equals the sum of coins in circulation, central bank notes outstanding, and demand deposits held by the public. The mint strikes the coins; the central bank issues the paper money and controls the volume of demand deposits. Demand deposits are the largest part of a country's money stock and the part that the central bank uses to control the total volume of money and credit in the country.

The central bank can create or destroy money by changing the amount of bank reserves. Table 7–3 shows how the central bank causes an expansion in the volume of loans and deposits. Suppose the central bank buys $100 in government securities from a bank, the first bank in Table 7–3. The central bank pays for the securities by crediting the reserves that the first bank has on deposit with the central bank. Step 1 in Table 7–3 shows the changes in the balance sheets of the first bank and the central bank that this transaction produces. Provided the first bank had only its required reserves before the transaction, it has $100 in excess reserves after the transaction; and it will lend that $100 to a customer, as shown in step 2, in order to maximize its profits. When the loan is spent, the deposits of the second bank increase by $100, provided the public always redeposits its extra money in the banking system. The second bank must keep $10 on reserve, assuming that 10 percent of deposits are required reserves, but it can lend an additional $90, as shown in step 3. When the $90 is redeposited in the third bank, $9.00 must be kept in reserves, and $81 can be lent to the public (step 4), which increases the deposits of the fourth bank (step 5).

The creation of excess reserves by the central bank produces a multiple expansion of deposits in the banking system. Each bank that receives an increase in its deposits is required to

Table 7-3   The Expansion of Demand Deposits (dollars)

Step 1

FIRST BANK		CENTRAL BANK	
Reserves + 100		Government	Bank
Government		securities + 100	reserves + 100
securities − 100			

Step 2

FIRST BANK	
Reserves − 100	
Loans + 100	

Step 3

SECOND BANK	
Reserves + 10	Deposits +100
Loans + 90	

Step 4

THIRD BANK	
Reserves + 9	Deposits + 90
Loans + 81	

Step 5

FOURTH BANK	
Reserves + 8.10	Deposits + 81
Loans +72.90	

keep only a fraction of them on reserve and can lend out the
rest. As funds are lent, spent, and redeposited, the total amount
of deposits increases, though at a diminishing rate. At each step
a fraction of the new deposits must go into reserves. The total
increase in reserves, loans, and deposits that can ultimately occur
is illustrated in Table 7–4. If the required reserve ratio is one-tenth
of deposits, total deposits can increase to a maximum of ten times

Table 7-4   The Multiple Expansion of Loans and Deposits (dollars)

	RESERVES	LOANS	DEPOSITS
Step 1	+ 100.00	− 100.00	
Step 2	− 100.00	+ 100.00	
Step 3	+ 10.00	+ 90.00	+ 100.00
Step 4	+ 9.00	+ 81.00	+ 90.00
Step 5	+ 8.10	+ 72.90	+ 81.00
.	.	.	.
.	.	.	.
.	.	.	.
Sum of all steps	+ 100.00	+ 900.00	+1,000.00

the initial increase in reserves. This can be calculated from the following formula:

$$\text{change in deposits} = \frac{\text{change in reserves}}{\text{required reserve ratio}}$$

Where an additional $100 in reserves is created and where the required reserve ratio is .10, the maximum change in deposits equals $1,000 (1,000 = 100 ÷ .10).

The maximum expansion of deposits occurs provided two conditions are met. First, banks must stay loaned up; that is, excess reserves must be lent to customers or used to buy securities. If banks are unwilling to lend or if the public is unwilling to borrow, excess reserves may accumulate and no expansion occur. However, excess reserves do not often build up far because banks can always buy Treasury bills, which are virtually riskless and earn interest. Second, the public must redeposit in the banking system every extra dollar it receives. There can be no leakage of money out of deposits into currency for hand-to-hand circulation or out of the country.

Bank reserves are sometimes called *high powered money*, because they can produce a multiple change in the total amount of money in the economy. The monetary policy of the central bank operates through bank reserves. If the central bank increases reserves, a multiple expansion of deposits occurs; if it reduces reserves, a multiple contraction occurs.

Monetary Policy Tools

Monetary policy refers to the actions taken by the central bank to regulate a country's stock of money, its volume of credit, and its rate of interest. The rate of interest and the volume of bank credit depend on the stock of money, which in turn is governed by the amount of bank reserves. An *easy money* policy exists when the central bank expands reserves, which pushes interest rates down; a *tight money* policy exists when reserves are restricted and, thus, interest rates increased. The central bank has three main tools that alter bank reserves: open market operations, the discount rate, and the required reserve ratio. In addition, the central bank can use moral suasion to convince banks to support its policy.

Transactions by the central bank in securities, usually government securities, are called *open market operations*. When the central bank purchases a bond, the reserves of commercial banks increase whether the bond is purchased directly from a bank, as in the previous example on fractional reserve banking, or from the public. In the first case, the central bank pays for the security by increasing bank reserves directly; in the second case, the central bank writes a check on itself that increases bank reserves indirectly, provided the private citizen who receives the check deposits it in a commercial bank. In both cases, an increase in bank reserves causes a multiple expansion of deposits. A sale of securities by the central bank reduces reserves. If the sale is to a commercial bank, its reserves at the central bank are reduced to pay for the security; if the sale is to a private citizen, bank reserves are reduced when the central bank receives a check drawn on a commercial bank. In summary, open market purchases increase bank reserves and expand the money stock; open market sales reduce reserves and contract the money stock.

The *discount rate* is the rate of interest that the central bank charges commercial banks. The term discount comes from the practice of deducting interest charges from the face value of a loan when it is made instead of adding the interest charges when it is due. For example, for a one-year loan with a face value of $100 discounted at 6 percent, the bank pays out $94 and is owed $100 at the end of the year. The discounted value of a loan is simply its present value. It was common in former times for one man to write an IOU to another, who would then sell that IOU to a commercial bank at a discount. The commercial bank could then rediscount the same IOU at the central bank, which would collect when the IOU came due. The discount rate, therefore, is sometimes called the rediscount rate and sometimes simply the bank rate. A commercial bank increases its reserves when it discounts a customer's IOU at the central bank or when it writes its own IOU to the central bank, but it pays interest on the reserves it borrows. When reserves rise above the required level, a multiple expansion of deposits tends to occur.

A commercial bank employs the principle of opportunity cost when it compares the discount rate with the market rate of interest. If the discount rate is below the market rate, the commercial bank can increase its profits by borrowing at the lower rate and lending at the higher rate. By raising the discount rate, the central bank makes such transactions unprofitable, so that commercial banks reduce their borrowing and their reserves, which produces a multiple contraction in deposits. Banks also borrow from the central bank when their reserves fall below the required proportion of deposits. Since this is a signal to the central bank that the commercial bank may be overextended, commercial banks avoid borrowing excessively from the central bank.

The Federal Reserve Bank has the authority to change the *required reserve ratio*, the ratio of required reserves to deposits. This powerful tool is infrequently used, because a small change in the required reserve ratio can produce a large change in deposits. Deposits equal reserves divided by the required reserve ratio. If reserves equal $10 billion, a decrease in the required reserve ratio from 10 to 9 percent allows deposits to rise from $100 to $111 billion $(100 = 10 \div .10; 111 = 10 \div .09)$. Such a large change in deposits is rarely necessary within a short period of time.

Moral suasion refers to written and spoken statements issued by the central bank to the general public and to commercial banks. These statements may concern broad issues like the state of the economy or narrower issues like lending to foreign customers, buying mortgages, or dealing with minority groups. While these statements do not force banks to respond as certainly as does a change in reserves, banks can not safely ignore these appeals altogether. The central bank always has more powerful tools at its disposal.

Open market operations are the most flexible and the most important monetary policy tool, because purchases and sales of government securities can be made frequently and in almost any amount. In contrast, the discount rate is only effective to the extent that commercial banks borrow from the central bank, while changes in the required reserve ratio have too great an impact on the money stock to be used frequently. Moral suasion is a useful, if not a powerful, addition to the tools of central banks.

Monetary Policy and Aggregate Demand

Monetary policy is used to combat such economic problems as unemployment, inflation, and disequilibrium in the balance of payments. Monetary policy deals with economic problems by changing aggregate demand, but its impact on aggregate demand is indirect and is effective only after a period of time. This is illustrated by the flow chart in Figure 7–2, which shows monetary policy tools at one end of the chain of causation, economic problems at the other end, and a number of links connecting the ends.

The central bank changes its monetary policy in response to changing economic conditions. A time lag ordinarily

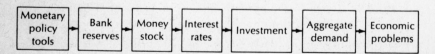

Figure 7-2 Monetary Policy and Economic Problems

occurs before the central bank changes its policy, because it will not act on one or two months of evidence. As a rule, it pursues a policy of "leaning against the wind." A rising price level or a widening balance-of-payments deficit calls for a tight money policy, while a rising rate of unemployment warrants an easy money policy.

Once the central bank recognizes that a policy change is appropriate, it will undertake to change commercial bank reserves with one or more of its main policy tools—open market operations, the discount rate, or the required reserve ratio. An increase in bank reserves tends to produce a multiple expansion of the money stock, provided banks lend out any excess reserves they receive and provided the public redeposits additional money in the banking system. A decrease in commercial bank reserves forces banks to call in loans or sell securities in order to meet their legal requirements. The central bank can always change commercial bank reserves relatively quickly if it wants to pursue a vigorous policy; and this will generally alter the stock of money within a short period of time as well.[3]

The liquidity preference theory explains how the supply of money affects the rate of interest: a change in the money supply tends to change the interest rate in the opposite direction. An easy money policy increases the cash balances of consumers, so that they hold more idle balances than they desire at the market rate of interest. They will, therefore, tend to buy bonds with their excess idle balances; this bids up the price of bonds and depresses the rate of interest. A tight money policy pushes interest rates up. Unless the economy is in the liquidity trap, the central bank can reduce interest rates; it can always increase the interest rate with a sufficiently strong policy.[4]

Investment varies inversely with the interest rate, because the quantity of new capital goods demanded increases as the cost of borrowing funds declines, as discussed in Chapter 4.

---

[3] If consumers increase their demand for goods and services as their cash balances increase, then the links in the chain of causation from monetary policy to aggregate demand may be different, consumption may replace investment, though the time lag may be no shorter than is illustrated in Figure 7-2. In order for consumer cash balances to increase, it should be noted, someone must first obtain more funds from the banking system. Either consumers must borrow more themselves or someone whose spending increases consumers' cash balances must borrow more, both of which are caused by lower interest rates. Thus, the interest rate is a critical link in the chain of causation.

[4] Since international capital flows respond to interest rate differentials, as discussed in Chapter 6, monetary policy tends to affect the balance of payments before it affects aggregate demand.

When the rate of return on new capital goods exceeds the rate of interest in financial markets, business enterprises can increase their profits by borrowing funds and acquiring additional plant and equipment. As investment increases, the rate of return on capital goods declines until it equals the rate of interest, at which point it is no longer profitable to increase investment. Thus, an easy money policy tends to increase investment, though it may take months to plan and perhaps years to build new capital goods. A tight money policy tends to decrease investment.

Investment has a multiple impact on aggregate demand. Additional investment increases the income of the people employed constructing new capital goods. Those people spend a portion of their additional income on consumer goods, as measured by their marginal propensity to consume. As consumption goes up, other people receive additional income, a portion of which they spend on consumption. A decrease in investment has the opposite effect on aggregate demand. The investment multiplier measures the response of aggregate demand to a change in investment, a response that takes time to occur. Finally, aggregate demand affects the amount of employment, the level of prices, and the balance of payments. These relationships are examined in the next three chapters.

UNEMPLOYMENT 8

Unemployment Defined

Unemployment, as defined in economic theory, exists when people who are willing to work at the current wage rate can not find employment. This is often called involuntary unemployment, which is distinct from the voluntary unemployment of retired workers and others who are not employed and not seeking employment. In principle, the labor force includes only people who are willing to work at market wages whether they are employed or not. The unemployment rate measures the percentage of the labor force that is unemployed.

Unemployment can be defined in terms of the supply

and demand curves in Figure 8–1, which assume that there is a single grade of labor and a single rate of wages. The supply curve shows how many hours people are willing to work at various wage rates. It slopes upward to the right indicating that the quantity of labor supplied increases as the wage rate rises; either more people join the labor force or more hours are worked by people already in the labor force. The demand curve shows how much labor business is willing to employ at alternative wage rates. It slopes downward because of the law of diminishing returns; output increases at a declining rate as additional labor is employed to work with a fixed amount of other inputs. The marginal product of labor declines; and, as was shown in Chapter 1, the value of the marginal product for labor (VMP) is the demand curve for labor in a competitive market. The quantity of labor demanded rises as the wage rate falls because profits increase as long as the extra revenue produced by a laborer exceeds his wage. Business enterprises maximize their profits where the wage equals the value of the marginal product of labor ($W = VMP$).

At the equilibrium wage rate (W_0), the quantity of labor demanded equals the quantity supplied; there is no unemployment. Above the equilibrium wage rate (W_1), a greater quantity of labor is supplied than is demanded; there is an excess supply of labor, that is, there is involuntary unemployment. Unemployment equals the difference between the quantity supplied and the quantity demanded ($Q_2 - Q_1$).

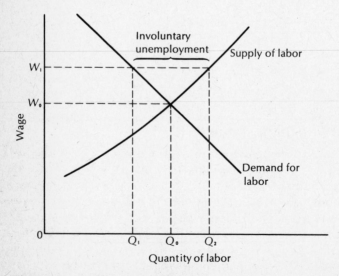

Figure 8-1   Involuntary Unemployment

Figure 8–1 is a simplification. Some unemployment always exists; the unemployment rate is never zero. Some people are always joining the labor force, quitting their jobs, or being dismissed, so that they are temporarily unemployed even though suitable jobs exist for them. The labor market is not a perfect mechanism that reaches equilibrium instantly. People do not have perfect knowledge about job vacancies, and they are not always sufficiently mobile to go where work is available. These market imperfections cause *frictional* unemployment. When only frictional unemployment exists, there is said to be full employment.

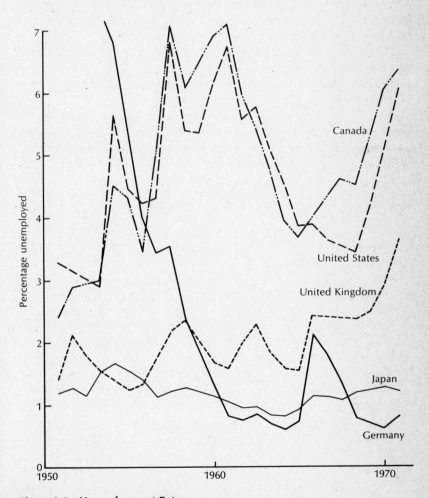

Figure 8-2 Unemployment Rates

Source: *U.N. Statistical Yearbook.*

Full employment corresponds to unemployment rates observed during periods of prosperity.

Unemployment rates for Canada, Germany, Japan, the United Kingdom, and the United States are charted in Figure 8–2 for the last two decades. Since each country collects its labor force statistics somewhat differently, these rates are not wholly comparable. Each country may also have a different level of frictional unemployment because of the nature of its labor market. For Canada and the United States, full employment appears to occur at about a 4 percent rate of unemployment, which is about the rate that prevailed during the peaks of the Korean and Vietnam wars, when jobs were readily available. For Germany and Japan, full employment corresponds to an unemployment rate that is about 1 percent of the labor force; for the United Kingdom, 2 percent unemployed appears to be the full employment rate. The rates of unemployment in all these countries have been above the frictional level from time to time, above 7 percent for Canada, Germany, and the United States. The periods of high unemployment in Figure 8–2 correspond to periods of falling or slowly increasing GNP per capita in Figure 2–1. These periodic high rates are called *cyclical unemployment* and are due to a deficient aggregate demand.

Why Unemployment Is a Social Problem

Unemployment is a social problem because it reduces the economic welfare of both the worker and society. The worker receives less income, while society produces fewer goods and services. A machine can be switched off when it is not needed and left idle for a week, a month, or a year. If it is properly maintained, it can be switched on again at some future time and used to produce as much as before. A laborer is not like a machine. When a laborer is idle, his life goes on; and, since his life is limited, what is not produced during his idle periods is lost forever. Temporary unemployment is a permanent waste.

Unemployment hurts the worker as well. Statistics are a poor measure of the loss in self-esteem, the distress to the family, and the disruption of lifetime plans that the unemployed suffer. Unemployment does not mean just a loss in income, no more sirloin steak, a repossessed color television set, or selling the car; it means despair for the future and fear of perpetual deprivation.

The employed as well as the unemployed suffer when people are unable to find work. They must bear the cost of unemployment compensation, expanded relief services, and even increased police protection. They may eventually find themselves unemployed, too, for society is composed of interdependent parts. Unemployment tends to create more unemployment as declining consumption expenditures generate a multiple contraction in aggregate demand. As an empirical rule, profits fall even more than wages during periods of declining demand, so that even the rich and powerful are affected by the spread of unemployment.

Employment and Aggregate Demand

Employment depends on the aggregate demand for goods and services. As additional labor is employed, output increases; but it is only profitable to increase output if the demand for goods and services increases. Once the level of aggregate demand is determined, the level of employment is determined. The relationship between aggregate demand, output, and employment is illustrated in Figure 8–3.

The 45-degree-line diagram, which reproduces Figure 3–4 from Chapter 3, shows how income and output are determined by aggregate demand. Income (Y) in constant dollars, which equals the constant dollar value of output, is measured along the horizontal axis; planned spending is measured in constant dollars along the vertical axis. An initial aggregate demand curve $(C+A_I)$ equals consumption (C) plus a given amount of autonomous spending (A_I) on investment, government purchases, and net exports. This spending is autonomous in the sense that it is assumed for the moment to be a constant amount. Since planned consumption increases as income increases, aggregate demand increases as well. The 45-degree line depicts the equilibrium condition in which aggregate demand $(C+A)$ equals income (Y). For the initial aggregate demand curve $(C+A_I)$, the equilibrium level of income and output is Y_I.

The diminishing returns diagram, which is based on Figure 1–4 from Chapter 1, shows that output increases at a diminishing rate as successive units of labor are brought into production. Output increases as more labor is employed, but it increases at a diminishing rate because more labor is working with a fixed quantity of the other factors of production—land and capital. An output of Y_I requires at least L_I laborers; and, if businesses maximize their profits, only L_I laborers will be employed. An increase in output requires more labor.

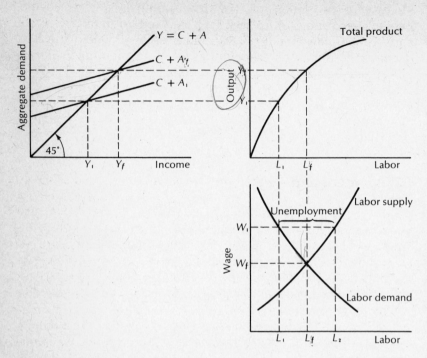

Figure 8-3   Unemployment and Aggregate Demand

The diagram for the demand and supply of labor is the same as Figure 8–1, which treats labor as a homogeneous aggregate. It supposes that the level of aggregate demand and, therefore, the volume of output have already been determined and that the quantity of labor employed is, thereby, also determined. Where L_1 labor is employed, the value of the marginal product (VMP) of the last laborer employed equals the wage rate (W_1). At the wage rate (W_1), however, a greater quantity of labor is supplied (L_2) than is demanded (L_1). An excess supply of labor exists, and there is involuntary unemployment.

Classical economists argued that involuntary unemployment exists because the market wage rate (W_1) is above the equilibrium or full employment wage rate and that a cut in wages would eliminate unemployment. J. M. Keynes disputed their conclusion by arguing that a cut in wages would eliminate unemployment only if it increased aggregate demand. Even though a cut in wages might temporarily induce employers to hire more labor and thereby increase labor income, unemployment would not be eliminated. Spending would tend to move out along the aggregate demand curve; but the aggregate demand curve would be the same as before; and the equilibrium level of income and output would be the same as before, so that employment would tend to fall back to its initial level. In order to increase employment, a cut in wages must shift the aggregate demand curve up.[1]

Unemployment and Economic Policy

An economic policy that increases aggregate demand will tend to eliminate unemployment. If autonomous spending rises from A_1 to A_f in Figure 8–3, income rises to the full employment level (Y_f) where L_f labor is demanded. At L_f the quantity of labor demanded equals the quantity supplied; there is no unemployment. The market wage becomes W_f, at which everyone willing to work can find a job. Both fiscal policy and monetary policy can be used to increase aggregate demand.

Fiscal Policy   The fiscal policy of the government sets the level of its expenditures and taxes. Government purchases of output are a component of aggregate demand and affect it directly; transfers to persons and taxes affect aggregate demand indirectly by altering disposable income. During a period of unemployment, the government can increase aggregate demand and reduce unemployment by increasing purchases, by increasing transfers, or by reducing taxes.

Deficit spending has the largest multiple impact on income, output, and employment (see Chapter 5). Not only is aggregate demand increased by the additional government spending, but it is increased by consumer spending, too. The households that receive extra income increase their spending by an amount determined by their marginal propensity to consume, which increases income, output, and employment further. The multiplier measures the total change in income due to a change in government purchases. However, if the government raises taxes to finance its extra expenditures, the expansionary effect on output and employment is reduced, because households have no extra disposable income to spend. The balanced budget mul-

---

[1] A wage cut could increase output in a few obscure and unlikely cases. For example, if prices fall as wages are cut, net exports tend to increase, provided the demand for imports and exports is sufficiently elastic. Since net exports are a component of aggregate demand, output tends to rise. Also, falling wages and prices tend to reduce the transactions demand for money as it takes fewer dollars to buy the same goods and services. Provided the stock of money does not fall, idle cash balances will accumulate, which will tend to reduce the interest rate, stimulate investment, and increase aggregate demand. Since wages and prices rarely fall, these cases are most unlikely.

tiplier is less than the deficit spending multiplier, as discussed in Chapter 5. Rather than increase taxes to finance additional expenditures, the government that seeks full employment should cut taxes in order to stimulate additional private spending. An increase in government transfer payments, such as unemployment compensation, also produces a multiple increase in income and output. The people receiving the transfers buy goods and services that are produced by others, who in turn increase their spending. Either cutting taxes or increasing transfers has a larger impact on GNP than a balanced budget. However, the size of the multiplier may be a poor criterion for fiscal policy.

The time required to implement fiscal policy can be an important constraint on its effectiveness. If new legislation is required, unemployment may continue for a year or more before any action is taken. First, policy makers must recognize and agree that unemployment has become unacceptably high. Second, a new bill must be drafted, hopefully with care, and passed by the legislature. In the case of a tax cut or increased relief, disposable income can be increased almost as soon as the government is authorized to act. For example, income tax withholdings can be reduced and welfare checks enlarged on very short notice. In the case of public works projects, however, time-consuming plans and contracts must be drawn up. Consider, for example, how much time it would take to build a new urban transportation system. The engineering plans and the acquisition of right-of-way would take years, by which time unemployment may not be the problem.

A *discretionary* policy, which requires explicit government action, can not take effect as quickly as an *automatic* policy, which requires neither recognition nor legislation by the government. Unemployment compensation rises automatically when workers are dismissed; income tax receipts fall automatically when income falls, so that the government tends to run a deficit. These automatic stabilizers are the first line of defense against unemployment, though they have rarely been sufficient by themselves. Discretionary action has generally been necessary to reduce unemployment.

Monetary Policy   The monetary policy of the central bank regulates the volume of money and credit in the economy. The principal tools of monetary policy are open market operations, the discount rate, and the required reserve ratio. These tools are used to alter the reserves of commercial banks, which produces a multiple change in the volume of money and credit. During a period of unemployment, the central bank can pursue an easy money policy to depress interest rates, encourage investment, increase output, and reduce unemployment.

The chain of causation from a change in monetary policy to its effect on unemployment is long and indirect. To combat unemployment, the central bank ordinarily purchases securities on the open market. Whether these securities are purchased from commercial banks or from the public, bank reserves tend to rise above requirements. Since excess reserves earn no interest, banks use these reserves to acquire interest-bearing IOUs by making loans or buying bonds. Provided these funds are redeposited in the banking system, the creation of excess reserves causes a multiple expansion of the money stock. An expansion of the money stock reduces interest rates, as explained by the liquidity preference theory. If financial markets were in equilibrium before the increase in the money stock, afterwards people would hold an excess of idle cash balances at the initial interest rate. Since the alternative to holding idle cash balances is holding interest-bearing bonds, people increase their demand for bonds, which bids up bond prices and pushes down the interest rate. The demand for newly produced capital goods is inversely related to the rate of interest, as discussed in Chapter 4. Therefore, when the interest rate falls, investment rises. Investment is a component of aggregate demand; thus, an increase in investment causes a multiple expansion of income and output. More output requires more labor. In this way, an easy money policy tends to reduce unemployment.

Monetary policy is more flexible than fiscal policy because the central bank has the authority to act on its own discretion within the limits of existing legislation. It can switch from a tight money to an easy money policy as soon as it recognizes that unemployment is too high. Once the central bank acts, however, the effect of its policy on unemployment is uncertain in timing and in magnitude.

The long chain of causation may be weak at many points. First, the creation of excess reserves will not expand the money stock by the maximum possible amount if funds are not redeposited in the banking system by the public. In recent years, large corporations have periodically deposited their funds abroad instead of at home. This reduces the reserves in the domestic banking system and may frustrate monetary policy. Second, if financial markets are in a liquidity trap, an increase in the money stock may not reduce interest rates far enough. This was a problem during the Great Depression, when banks preferred to hold idle excess reserves rather than interest-bearing IOUs, but it has not been a difficulty since World War II. Third, the demand for capital goods may be inelastic in response to a change in the interest rate. If investors do not respond sufficiently to a decline in the interest rate, investment will not raise aggregate demand to the full employment level. This has often been the case during depressions when low profits have caused businessmen to be pessimistic about the future. Fourth, as an empirical observation, interest rates on long-term bonds, which are used to finance new capital projects, rarely fall quickly; even if they did, it would take as much as a year or more for private corporations to plan, finance, and build new capital structures and equipment. Thus, within a short period of time, monetary policy probably has little effect on unemployment.

If unemployment were the only problem facing the government, it would probably pursue both an expansionary fiscal policy and an easy money policy. If it had to choose between the two policies, it would have to weigh the greater flexibility of monetary policy against the greater certainty of fiscal policy. In the last decade, however, the choice of an appropriate policy to reduce unemployment has been strongly affected by the simultaneous existence of inflation and a balance-of-payments disequilibrium.

Other Causes of Unemployment

Involuntary unemployment can be caused by a deficient aggregate demand or by imperfections in the labor market. A deficient aggregate demand is the main cause of unemployment during depressions. A cyclical decline in demand increases unemployment, while an upswing in aggregate demand reduces unemployment. Unemployment also occurs when the size of the labor force increases more rapidly than the growth of GNP provides new jobs. Aggregate demand is deficient, even though the immediate cause of the unemployment is an increase in the number of people willing to work. Imperfect knowledge and imperfect mobility of labor cause frictional unemployment, which exists even at the peak of economic activity. Market imperfections tend to aggravate the problem of unemployment when there is a change in seasons, a change in technology, or a change in the demand for particular commodities.

Fiscal policy and monetary policy can reduce cyclical unemployment by maintaining aggregate demand near the full employment level; they can also counteract unemployment due to an increase in the labor force by stimulating economic growth. To a certain extent, frictional unemployment can be reduced by the efforts of the government employment service, which provides laborers with information about job vacancies. Relocation grants have also been paid to laborers from time to time to induce them to move where more jobs are available. However, these policies may not effectively reduce seasonal or structural unemployment.

Seasonal unemployment arises from the nature of production in industries such as agriculture and construction and from the spending patterns of consumers at times such as Christmas and Easter. While little can be done about seasonal spending patterns and less about the weather, counterseasonal government spending or transfers can reduce seasonal unemployment. Canada and Norway, for example, have used special grants to encourage winter construction.

Structural unemployment occurs when there is an excess supply in particular labor markets, but not necessarily in all labor markets. The substitution of capital for labor can produce technological unemployment, so that particular types of labor are redundant. When the diesel locomotive replaced the steam engine and when the mechanical cotton picker replaced the field hand, thousands of workers were no longer needed. A shift in demand from one commodity to another—from coal to gas, for example—can also produce local unemployment. The same problem arises when one region of the country, such as New England, grows more slowly than the rest, or when one part of the labor force, such as teenage workers, grows more rapidly than the rest. Government relocation and retraining programs are used to combat structural unemployment, since policies directed at aggregate demand would be rather ineffective.

INFLATION

Inflation Defined and Measured

Inflation is defined as a persistent rise in the average level of prices. An average of prices must be calculated in order to determine whether inflation has occurred, because some prices fall as others rise. While inflation tends to increase wages, salaries, interest rates, and other factor payments, inflation is measured by product prices and not factor incomes, because technical progress also tends to increase incomes. The growth of wages, profits, or other factor payments due to improved methods of production should not be confused with inflation.

Inflation is ordinarily measured by an index number, which is a weighted average of prices. A price index compares the cost of purchasing a particular bundle of goods in a base period (year) with the cost of purchasing the same goods in other periods. The index number for the base period is typically set equal to 100.0, so that prices in other periods are expressed as a percentage of prices in the base period. For example, in Figure 9–1 the price index for each country equals 100.0 in 1963. The individual products covered by the index are assigned weights that reflect their relative importance in the index.

While price indexes can be constructed in a variety of ways, the Laspeyres index is the most widely used method. It weights the components of the price index by the quantities purchased in a particular period (year). These weights do not change

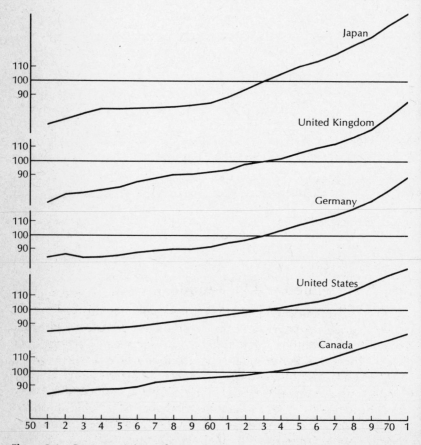

Figure 9-1   Consumer Price Indexes

Source: *U.N. Statistical Yearbook.*

Table 9-1 Prices and Quantities of Food

	BEEF PRICE (cents)	BEEF QUANTITY (pounds)	MILK PRICE (cents)	MILK QUANTITY (quarts)	BREAD PRICE (cents)	BREAD QUANTITY (loaves)
1960	40	100	20	300	18	200
1970	70	80	25	350	26	230

over time, unless the whole basis of computing the index is revised. Such an index is computed below from the data in Table 9–1 on the assumption that 1960 is both the comparison base (the year in which the index equals 100.0) and the weight base (the year from which the constant quantities are taken). In constructing the Laspeyres index, the weights—the quantities of beef, milk, and bread—remain at their 1960 levels; only the prices change: from 40 to 70 cents, 20 to 25 cents, and 18 to 26 cents.

$$P_{1960} = \frac{40 \times 100 + 20 \times 300 + 18 \times 200}{40 \times 100 + 20 \times 300 + 18 \times 200} \times 100$$

$$= \frac{13,600}{13,600} \times 100$$

$$= 100.0$$

$$P_{1970} = \frac{70 \times 100 + 25 \times 300 + 26 \times 200}{40 \times 100 + 20 \times 300 + 18 \times 200} \times 100$$

$$= \frac{19,700}{13,600} \times 100$$

$$= 144.9$$

Thus, it would cost 44.9 percent more in 1970 to purchase the same quantities of goods purchased in 1960.

The rate of inflation is expressed by the percentage increase in the price level per year. A slow and steady increase in prices of 1 or 2 percent a year is *creeping* inflation; a more rapid increase is sometimes called *galloping* inflation; and a very rapid rise in prices—say, 20 percent or more a year—is called *hyperinflation*. Prices in Germany increased over 100 percent a year after World War I and at the end of World War II. A fall in the general level of prices is called *deflation*. Figure 9–1 charts the consumer price index (CPI) for Canada, West Germany, Japan, the United Kingdom, and the United States. These consumer price indexes include goods and services that are purchased by a representative consumer in each country. They show that all five countries have experienced inflation in most years. For some years prices were merely creeping up; generally they have risen more rapidly, but not so rapidly as to be considered hyperinflation.

Why Inflation Is a Problem

Inflation becomes an important problem when it disrupts the economy. When prices are expected to rise by a small amount, people take inflation into account as they plan and contract for the future; otherwise their plans are sure to go awry. Creeping inflation should not surprise anyone today, but a sudden rise in prices of 5, 6, or more percentage points a year tends to reallocate income, to complicate planning, and to frighten people with the prospect of a loss in real income. Hyperinflation can lead to hoarding and severe shortages.

Periodic spurts of inflation have been the most serious type of inflation in industrialized countries since the end of World War II. Unlike unemployment, this sort of inflation does not reduce the total volume of goods and services in a country; rather, it allocates income and, therefore, the ability to purchase goods and services in a manner different from that which people expected or for which they planned. Some people are worse off, but others are better off because of inflation. For example, debtors benefit at the expense of their creditors. If during a period of relatively stable prices a man borrowed $1,000 at 5 percent and if within the year prices rose 7 percent, he would actually owe a sum of money that was worth less than what he borrowed. Similarly, a couple that retires on a pension that provides a fixed money income per year will become poorer and poorer as prices rise. A labor union that signs a long-term contract could face the same problem.

While inflation tends to reallocate income, it is not easy to identify which groups benefit and which groups suffer. Creditors may recover their losses, since interest rates typically rise during periods of inflation. Although pensioners realize less real income from their fixed pension payments, many also own real estate, stocks, and other property that can increase in value during periods of inflation. Unions will generally try to regain the real income that they have lost when they negotiate new contracts. However, many individuals undoubtedly do suffer a loss in real income during periods of inflation.

The political outcry against inflation may be due as much to the fear of a loss in real income as to the actual loss. Plans based on earlier price expectations are thrown into doubt. When prices rise rapidly, a person knows for certain that a dollar buys less, but he can not know whether his income will rise

Increased cost of transactions.

apace. Even when income is rising more rapidly than prices, people sometimes see only the rise in prices and feel poorer.

Hyperinflation prompts consumers and producers to buy now rather than later, to buy at current prices rather than at future prices that they expect to be much higher. Although it is only prudent for the individual to stock up on sugar, shoes, clothing, and other goods that are easily stored, hoarding can be disastrous for the economy as a whole. Households that need food, clothing, and other goods may not be able to buy them. Stores may be empty if goods have been hoarded. Manufacturers may also have difficulty buying particular materials, even though enough are available, if other companies have hoarded more than they need. Thus, some factories may be forced to cut back production or even shut down.

Hyperinflation can become self-perpetuating once it begins, if the government permits it to continue. On the one hand, the demand for hoards is added to the demand for current consumption, which tends to bid prices up. On the other hand, shortages obstruct production, which tends to reduce supply and increase prices further. Most cases of hyperinflation have been associated with major wars, such as the American Civil War or the two world wars, and have been the result of extraordinary deficit spending by the government.

Excess Demand Inflation

Excess demand inflation occurs when aggregate demand pushes against the capacity of the economy to produce goods and services. It typically occurs during the prosperity phase of the business cycle or during wartime. Indeed, most of the major spurts of inflation that have occurred in this century have been associated with wars: World War I, World War II, the Korean War, the war in Vietnam. On each of these occasions, the government has increased its expenditures on military equipment, supplies, and personnel without an equal decrease in private aggregate spending occurring elsewhere. In order to shift resources from the production of peacetime to wartime goods, the government has had to bid resources away from consumers and businesses. This has created an aggregate excess demand that has tended to pull prices up.

The effect of an excess demand for one commodity can be illustrated with the supply and demand diagram in Figure 9–2. The supply curve slopes upward to the right because of the law of diminishing returns. Within a short period of time, the stock of plant and equipment can not be greatly increased. Output can be increased by using more labor and materials, but it

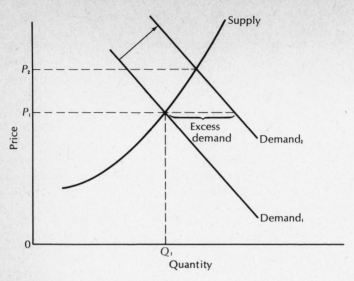

Figure 9-2   Supply and Demand

increases at a diminishing rate. Each extra unit of output requires a greater quantity of labor and materials. Thus, the marginal cost of production rises as output increases. Since a profit-maximizing corporation will not produce an extra unit of output unless the price covers its cost, the supply curve is upward sloping. The demand curves are downward sloping.

The equilibrium price is determined where the quantity supplied equals the quantity demanded. Given the supply curve and the initial demand curve (Demand$_1$), the equilibrium price is P_1. During the upswing of a business cycle or during wartime, the demand curve shifts upward to the right (Demand$_2$). At the old price (P_1), there is an excess demand; a greater quantity is demanded than is supplied. Those buyers who are willing to pay more than the initial price bid the price up to a new and higher level. An excess demand for goods and services in general causes inflation.

Aggregate excess demand is illustrated in terms of the 45-degree-line diagram in Figure 9–3. Income in constant dollars appears on the horizontal axis; consumer plus autonomous spending in constant dollars appears on the vertical axis. The 45-degree line shows the potential equilibrium points where income equals total spending. Suppose that the productive capacity of the economy is strictly limited at the full employment level of output (Y_f), which appears as a vertical line in the diagram. Where aggregate demand equals the full employment level of income ($Y_f = C + A_f$), neither unemployment nor inflation occurs. However, if total spending exceeds the productive capacity of

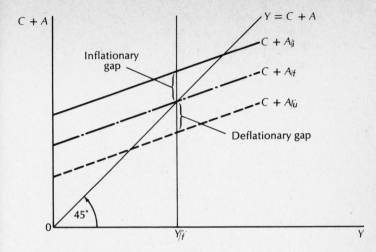

Figure 9-3   The Inflationary Gap

the nation, as it does where aggregate demand is $C + A_i$, an inflationary gap develops, and prices tend to rise. In terms of the supply and demand diagram, an excess demand exists at the old price level for goods and services in general. In the opposite case, where spending is below the full employment level, a deflationary gap and unemployment occur.

The inflationary gap is most obvious during wartime, particularly if the government takes no steps to reduce private spending. The enlarged government spending is an extra source of income to consumers, who tend to increase their spending in competition with the government. Even if the government were to raise taxes to pay for a war, inflation would tend to occur. Consumers could pay the taxes with their extra income and spend as much as before, while the military purchases would be a clear addition to aggregate demand. As a rule, governments run deficits to finance wars because the public is unwilling to pay enough taxes. The government tries to persuade consumers to buy bonds instead of goods and services. If this fails, as it has from time to time, the government can always print money to pay the army and the munitions industry. Printing money is simply an extreme form of deficit financing, one which quickly converts moderate inflation into hyperinflation.[1]

---

[1] Printing money to finance a deficit increases the money stock in the economy, but it has quite a different effect on the economy than an increase in bank deposits. An increase in bank money affects aggregate demand indirectly by way of its influence on the rate of interest. Printing money to buy war materials increases aggregate demand directly, because government purchases are a component of aggregate demand.

The inflationary gap diagram shows how an increase in autonomous spending can produce a general excess demand, but it does not show the response of prices to the inflationary gap. It is an oversimplification to suppose that inflation occurs only when aggregate demand exceeds the productive capacity of the economy and that unemployment occurs only when spending is below the full employment level. The productive capacity of the economy is not an inelastic and strictly limited level of output.

The rate of inflation produced by a general excess demand depends on how rapidly costs rise and on how rapidly productive capacity increases. Within a short period of time, productive capacity is not restricted to a definite quantity of goods and services but is more or less elastic. As the supply and demand diagram illustrates, costs rise as output increases, but output can still increase. As demand shifts out, prices rise. Over a longer period of time, productive capacity grows, and the supply curve shifts out. Aggregate demand and aggregate supply enter a race in which the winner decides the rate of inflation.

Economic Policy and Excess Demand Inflation

Both fiscal and monetary policy can be used to combat inflation by reducing aggregate demand. The policies that reduce demand during periods of inflation are the opposite of those that stimulate spending during periods of unemployment. Since expansionary policies are applied during depressions and restrictive policies during prosperity, the total policy over the course of the business cycle is *countercyclical*. The object of countercyclical policy is to hold aggregate demand at the point where there is neither unemployment nor inflation, at $C + A_f$ in Figure 9–3.

Fiscal policy reduces aggregate demand by cutting government purchases, increasing taxes, or diminishing transfer payments to persons. Smaller government purchases reduce aggregate demand directly, while higher taxes and lower transfer payments reduce disposable income, which decreases private spending. The multiplier downward tends to be larger for a reduction in government purchases than for an increase in taxes or a decrease in transfers, as discussed in earlier chapters. With a countercyclical fiscal policy, the government tends to run a surplus during prosperous times and a deficit during depressed times.

The progressive income tax is an automatic stabilizer that counteracts inflation. Every dollar spent is received by someone, so that someone receives a higher money income as soon as prices rise. The income tax is calculated as a percentage of money income, and that percentage rises as money income rises. For example, a household earning $10,000 a year may pay 15 percent, or $1,500, in taxes. If inflation increases its income to $15,000, it may have to pay 25 percent, or $3,750, in taxes. Thus, tax receipts tend to rise even faster than money income, and this tends to hold inflation in check.

Monetary policy can also be used to counter inflation. A tight money policy is formally the opposite of an easy money policy, though it tends to be more effective. An easy money policy is permissive and encourages expansion; a tight money policy is more forceful. Low interest rates stimulate investment only if profit expectations are strong, which they typically are not during a depression. High interest rates reduce the profitability of new investment whether businessmen are optimistic or pessimistic.

Open market sales to either the public or commercial banks are the main tight money policy tool of the central bank. A sale of securities by the central bank to the public, for example, is ordinarily paid for by a check drawn on a commercial bank, which the central bank clears by drawing down the reserves of that commercial bank. If the banking system had no excess reserves before, it has deficient reserves after the open market sale. That deficiency must be corrected on pain of bankruptcy by calling in loans or by selling off securities, either of which produces a multiple contraction in the volume of money and credit. The contraction in the money stock reduces idle cash balances, so that the public finds itself holding less cash at the current rate of interest than it desires. It will, therefore, sell bonds; this pushes down bond prices and increases the rate of interest. As the rate of interest rises, marginal investments in plant and equipment become unprofitable. The profit motive leads corporations and other investors to purchase fewer new capital goods, which reduces aggregate demand by a multiple. In the extreme case, the central bank can reduce the stock of money so severely that it is not even adequate for transactions purposes. No doubt many railroads, manufacturers, retailers, households, and others would be bankrupt before that point could be reached.

A sufficiently large reduction in bank reserves reduces aggregate demand more rapidly than an equally large expansion in reserves increases aggregate demand. A tight money policy can force banks to call in loans that companies need in order to do business—in order to purchase goods and materials and to employ labor. Since a large percentage of bank loans mature within 60 to 90 days, a tight money policy can take effect within as short a time as a quarter of a year and certainly within a year.

By restricting the volume of credit and increasing interest rates, a restrictive policy makes many business plans unprofitable, even impossible. In July 1973, for example, some short-term interest rates in West Germany reached 30 to 40 percent. Few capital goods earn as high a rate of return. An easy money policy merely encourages additional spending by making credit available and by reducing interest rates; it creates the opportunity for greater profits but does not force people to increase their spending.

Monetary policy is more often used to combat inflation than unemployment, in part because it can reduce aggregate demand more quickly than it can increase it and in part because central bankers have traditionally been more concerned with the purchasing power of money than with the labor force. Since central banks have the authority to restrict the volume of money and credit, they can move against inflation more quickly than budgetary authorities, who must obtain special legislation in order to pursue a deliberately restrictive fiscal policy.

Monetary policy can also act as an automatic stabilizer on the upswing of the business cycle or during a period of inflation, if the central bank does not let the stock of money grow in step with the dollar volume of transactions. When the money value of purchases increases, whether from an expansion of output or an increase in prices, the transactions demand for money increases. If the stock of money does not grow as fast, idle cash balances are reduced, which pushes up interest rates. Rising interest rates tend to check investment demand and, thereby, aggregate demand. Over the course of the business cycle, interest rates tend to rise and fall with aggregate demand, because the demand for transactions balances rises and falls with total spending.

Inflation with Unemployment

Inflation and unemployment often exist side-by-side as a glance at Figure 9–1 on inflation and Figure 8–2 on unemployment clearly demonstrates. Unemployment has often been above the frictional level during the last two decades for all five countries; some inflation has occurred in almost every year. A rough relation exists between the rate of unemployment and the rate of inflation.

The Phillips curve[2] (named after A. W. Phillips, a

---

[2] A. W. Phillips, "The Relation Between Unemployment and the Rate of Change of Money Wage Rates in the United Kingdom, 1861-1957," *Economica* 25 (December 1958), 283–299.

British economist), Figure 9–4, shows the relation between the unemployment rate and the percentage change in money wages. The unemployment rate is a measure of the excess supply of labor, the quantity by which labor supply exceeds labor demand at a given wage rate. When unemployment is low, employers bid against one another for the available labor force. Employers increase their demand for labor as output increases; as output approaches the full employment level, where only frictional unemployment exists, one employer must attract labor away from other employers by offering higher wages. Thus, the percentage increase in wages accelerates as unemployment falls. When unemployment is high, competition forces labor to accept smaller wage increases. In Figure 9–4, the money wage rate increases at 7 percent a year when unemployment is 3 percent; but when unemployment is 7 percent, money wages rise only 2 percent a year.

The Phillips curve is an empirical measure of the inverse relation between the unemployment rate and the per-

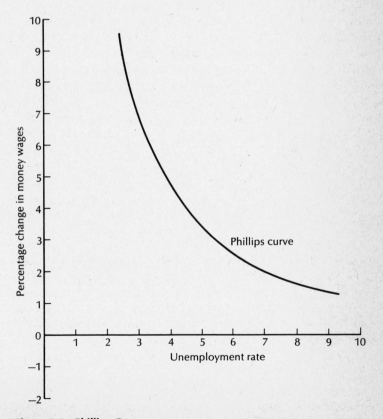

Figure 9-4 Phillips Curve

centage change in money wage rates. It is not a theory of inflation, but it does indicate how unemployment and inflation can exist at the same time. Labor productivity, the volume of output per employee, increases over time because of capital accumulation and technical progress. If it rises at a slower rate than wages, product prices will tend to rise; that is, if wages rise by 7 percent a year while output per worker rises by 3 percent a year, labor costs per unit of output will rise by 4 percent a year. An increase in the labor cost of producing a unit of output shifts the product supply curve up and tends to increase product prices. But why should wages increase more rapidly than labor productivity?

In terms of the inflationary gap diagram, wages tend to rise more rapidly than labor productivity when there is a general excess demand in the product market; the line of causation runs from product prices to wage rates. This is called *demand-pull inflation*. However, the line of causation could run the other way—wages could push up prices. This is called *cost-push inflation*, and it can be explained by several hypotheses: monopoly power, sticky wages, sectoral shifts in demand, service industry inflation, foreign inflation, and shortages in commodity markets.

The monopoly power of labor unions is one of the most popular explanations of inflation. A labor union is a monopoly when it represents all the electricians, all the truck drivers, or all the steelworkers in a particular market. As a monopoly, however, its power to gain wage increases is not unlimited. It may face a strong and well-organized group of employers trying to hold wages down. If not, if the employers are weak or if they can pass wage increases along to their customers, the union will still face a downward sloping demand curve for the services of its members. Too large a wage increase will reduce the quantity of labor demanded, and union members will be thrown out of work. To be effective, the union must choose a wage and employment package that will be acceptable to its membership.

Whether unions cause inflation is an empirical question that can be answered only by reference to the facts, facts which are not easily interpreted. Sometimes unions appear to be the devil behind rising prices when in fact they are merely trying to regain lost ground. When a union signs a contract for two or three years in the expectation that prices will not rise, it may be disappointed. A war may break out, create a general excess demand, pull prices up, and reduce the expected income of union members. When the old contract expires and a new one is negotiated, the union will often try to win a settlement that increases wages enough to compensate for the fact that prices have already risen. Such settlements tend to push prices up further, so that inflation continues well past the period of excess demand.

Giant corporations as well as trade unions have been accused of causing inflation from time to time, because they also have a degree of monopoly power. However, the monopoly power of private companies probably can not explain the periodic spurts of inflation that have occurred in this century, not only because these periods have usually been associated with wartime expenditures, but also because monopoly power does not come in spurts. Why would large corporations in general or trade unions in general choose one period rather than another to exercise their power? Creeping inflation is not easily explained by monopoly power either, because giant corporations have not increased their profits and unions have not increased their wages relative to other income categories over the course of time.

Governments, not private corporations, give the best example of inflation caused by monopoly power. The Organization of Petroleum Exporting Countries (OPEC), a government-operated international cartel or monopoly, used its power to raise oil prices in 1973 and 1974; and this had an inflationary impact on oil importing countries.

Creeping inflation can be explained by the downward rigidity of money wages, what are sometimes called *sticky* wages. Laborers, union and nonunion alike, vigorously resist wage cuts, so that money wages tend to be sticky downward, but flexible upward. Over the course of the business cycle, money wages rise during periods of prosperity, when there is an excess demand, but do not fall during depressions, when there is an excess supply of labor. Once prices have risen to a given level, they do not recede when aggregate demand declines; they merely pause and then resume their rise as soon as aggregate demand rises again. Thus, the average level of product prices tends to creep up over time.

Sticky wages also explain why inflation occurs when demand shifts from one sector of the economy to another. Suppose, for example, that demand shifts toward the capital goods sector and away from the consumer goods sector. An excess demand for capital goods tends to increase their prices, while excess capacity in the consumer goods industries does not force those prices down because of the downward rigidity of wages. Since sectoral shifts in demand are inherent in a dynamic economy, so is inflation. A sudden shift in demand could produce a sharp rise in the average level of product prices, even though there was not a general excess demand. The sectoral shift theory of inflation was advanced by Charles L. Schultze to explain the rise in prices during the late 1950s.[3]

The service industries, including government services, have grown more rapidly than the goods producing industries. This long-term shift in demand has caused prices to creep up for a special reason. In the goods producing industries, technical progress keeps prices from rising in step with money wages. Each year output per worker and, therefore, real income per worker increases as more capital and better methods of production are employed. In the service industries, labor productivity does not improve as rapidly; or, if it does, the improvement is not easily measured. Inflation in the service industries involves both a measurement problem and an allocation problem.

Medical services illustrate the measurement problem. Medical services have improved. Fewer people die at an early age because of improved drugs, surgery, and other health services. An accurate price index of medical services should be adjusted for quality changes. By analogy, if a new model car has an eight- instead of a six-cylinder engine or if it has four doors instead of two, an adjustment to the price index should take these improvements into account. However, price indexes generally assume that medical services have not improved, so that the price of medical services increases with every increase in the incomes of doctors, nurses, and other health workers. An improvement in the quality of health care is, in part, confounded with an increase in the price of medical services of a given quality.

The allocation problem may cause the average level of product prices to rise by 1 to 2 percent a year. If the prices of both goods and services were held constant, wages would rise in the goods producing industries as productivity improved; but wages would remain constant in the service industries, where productivity is constant, as measured. This would attract labor away from the production of services toward the production of goods, which is not the allocation that consumers demand. If the price of goods does not fall, market forces push costs up in the service industries and cause creeping inflation.

Inflation abroad can cause inflation at home. Both imports and exports are affected. A rise in the price of foreign goods increases domestic prices directly when they are imported and sold at home, provided the exchange rate is fixed. A domestic producer who has the alternative of selling at home or abroad

---

[3] Charles L. Schultze, *Recent Inflation in the United States*, Study Paper no. 1 for Joint Economic Committee, Study of Employment, Growth, and Price Levels (Washington, D.C.: U.S. Government Printing Office, 1959).

will tend to raise prices as well. If he can get a higher price abroad than at home, why should he sell for less at home? Domestic purchasers must match the higher foreign prices. This is why inflation in one major trading area tends to become worldwide. The inflation of both the Korean and Vietnamese wars affected most of the countries of the world, irrespective of their role in these wars. The inflation of the early 1970s was also worldwide.

Commodity shortages occurred simultaneously in several markets in 1972–1973 and were a major cause of inflation. The corn crop failed in the United States because of blight, and the wheat crop failed in the Soviet Union because of drought. As a result, the world prices of corn and wheat rose dramatically. This forced up the prices of beef, chicken, and other animals that are fed on grain. The disruption of copper production in Zambia and Chile had the same effect on copper prices, and the closing of zinc smelters in the United States to protect the environment caused zinc prices to rise. Since all of these shortages occurred when the Western European, U.S., and Japanese economies were running close to capacity, inflation was particularly severe.

While the inflationary gap diagram, Figure 9–3, assumes that no inflation occurs up to the point of full employment and no unemployment during periods of inflation, in fact inflation and unemployment often exist together. The Phillips curve in Figure 9–4 shows that a trade-off exists between the rate of unemployment and the change in money wages: the lower the rate of unemployment, the greater the rise in money wages. A related trade-off is often assumed to exist between unemployment and inflation. This implies that the government must be prepared to accept a degree of unemployment and a degree of inflation and that it can achieve greater price stability only at the cost of more unemployment. An optimum policy produces that mix of inflation and unemployment which best satisfies (or least dissatisfies) society. However, both prices and unemployment are affected by a variety of forces that can cause the Phillips curve to shift. For example, in the early 1970s the extraordinary rise in the prices of raw materials and foodstuffs caused a worldwide inflation without causing a large increase in the demand for labor, so that the Phillips curve shifted up.

Incomes Policy

An *incomes policy* involves the direct regulation of prices and incomes by the national government. When inflation and unemployment are unacceptably high at the same time, countercyclical monetary and fiscal policies can not solve both problems. An expansionary policy aggravates the problem of inflation, while a restrictive policy aggravates the problem of unemployment. An incomes policy makes it possible to deal with both problems. Controlling prices and incomes holds inflation in check, at the same time that expansionary monetary and fiscal policies increase output and reduce unemployment. An incomes policy tends to shift the Phillips curve toward the origin of the graph in Figure 9–4.

     An incomes policy faces two economic problems: it requires a large bureaucracy to administer, and it tends to misallocate resources. These problems often generate substantial political opposition after, if not before, an incomes policy is employed.

     The administration of all the prices and incomes in an economy is a vast undertaking, though it is not impossible. A single supermarket, for example, may sell 10,000 to 15,000 different items, each of which may pass through several hands—farmer, canner, jobber, retailer—before it reaches the final consumer. At each point in the channel of production and distribution, foodstuffs sell at different prices. Furthermore, prices vary from city to city and from time to time. Oranges cost more in Fairbanks, Alaska, than in Orlando, Florida; and they cost more everywhere when a frost hits Florida. Thus, in order to regulate food prices exactly, the government might have to set a million prices, each of which should involve careful study. The clothing, housing, and transportation markets—not to mention the labor market—are of comparable complexity. The government can not establish a bureaucracy that is large enough and competent enough to administer all the prices and incomes in the economy on short notice.

     Prices and incomes must eventually be changed, for otherwise resources will be grossly misallocated. Prices help to allocate resources. High prices attract products and factor services; low prices force them away. The self-interest of the producer or the resource owner prompts him to sell his goods or services where they fetch the highest prices. In this way the market mechanism tends to eliminate a shortage, which is but another name for an excess demand. When an excess demand exists, prices rise until a new equilibrium is established; as prices rise, the quantity supplied increases and the quantity demanded decreases until the two quantities are equal. A surplus, or an excess supply, produces the opposite result: prices fall, the quantity supplied is reduced, and the quantity demanded increases until a new equilibrium is established. A price freeze that does not permit prices and incomes to change will soon create shortages in some places and surpluses in others, indicating that resources are misallocated.

With prices fixed, shortages and surpluses could arise for many reasons: a change in consumer preferences, a crop failure, a strike, or something else. If consumers decide to move from the country to the city, a surplus of old houses will exist in rural areas while a shortage exists in urban areas. Who gets the available urban housing? If the production of a commodity is reduced by a crop failure or a strike, who gets the available supply? With prices fixed, commodities are not sold to the highest bidder.

The United States, British, and Canadian governments have all experimented with various incomes policies, none of which has been entirely successful. These policies can be ranked according to their administrative complexity.

First, virtually no administrative machinery is needed to establish voluntary guidelines that are not legally binding. The government simply announces that wage and price increases in excess of certain norms (say, 6 percent for wages and 3 percent for prices) are inflationary and contrary to the public interest. However, guidelines without legal sanctions have not been very effective. Individuals pursue their own interests rather than the public interest, and prices continue to rise.

Second, a wage and price freeze that is legally binding requires only the simplest police surveillance to administer. Price increases are easily discovered, and fines are easily imposed. Wages and prices could be frozen forever if the penalties were sufficiently severe. However, the more severe the penalties, the greater will be the political opposition to a freeze; and the longer a freeze lasts, the greater will be the misallocation of resources. Thus, wage and price freezes have generally been temporary.

Third, an incomes policy can be applied to only very large corporations and unions, which can be required to report to a council (board or commission) and obtain approval for increases in prices, wages, dividends, and so on. Confining the review procedure to only large corporations and unions minimizes the administrative work of the government. This type of incomes policy is well-suited to cost-push inflation that is caused by monopoly power. However, the major spurts of inflation that have occurred in this century have been caused by excess demand in general or in particular industries, not by monopoly power. Restricting price and wage increases by large corporations and unions during a period of excess demand inflation causes them to suffer a decline in real income relative to smaller businesses and nonunion workers. Inflation is checked in some places, but it continues in the uncontrolled parts of the economy.

Fourth, prices and incomes can be regulated by a comprehensive system of controls, such as were used during World War II. This requires a massive bureaucracy; for not only must all prices and incomes be set, but physical quantities of goods and services must be allocated as well. During a period of excess demand, a greater quantity of goods and services is demanded at the controlled prices than suppliers are willing to sell. During World War II, this difficulty was solved by directly allocating war materials and by rationing essential consumer goods. Since the market was not permitted to allocate goods to the highest bidder, another system of allocation was developed. Businesses needed government approval and consumers needed ration coupons to buy what they wanted.

When the rate of inflation and the rate of unemployment are unacceptably high, the government faces a dilemma. Aggregative monetary and fiscal policies will tend to increase either the rate of inflation or the rate of unemployment. For this reason, an incomes policy appears attractive, but its attractiveness diminishes the longer and more strongly the policy is pursued. Unions object when their wages are held down, and they may strike. Corporations object when profits are restricted, and they may reduce the quality of the products they sell in order to disguise an increase in prices. Consumers object when shortages occur, and they may prefer to buy on the blackmarket at illegal prices. A forceful incomes policy can be used only for a short period of time before it produces substantial economic and political opposition.

BALANCE
OF
PAYMENTS

Surpluses and Deficits

The balance-of-payments account records all the transactions between one country and the rest of the world during a given time period, such as a year. These transactions involve imports and exports of currently produced goods and services, unilateral transfers by persons and by governments, and financial transactions, including official operations in the foreign exchange market. When all these transactions are considered together, the whole account balances (subject to errors and omissions) as shown in Table 10–1. However, a surplus or deficit may exist for any particular type of transaction, and it may be a cause for con-

Table 10-1   Balance-of-Payments Account, 1973 (billions of dollars)

TRANSACTIONS	RECEIPTS	PAYMENTS	BALANCE
Merchandise	10.1	12.3	
Services	6.2	5.4	
Balance on Net Export Account			−1.4
Transfers	.1	1.1	
Long-term capital	2.1	4.8	
Basic Balance			−5.1
Short-term capital:			
Nonliquified short-term capital	4.2	0.9	
Liquidity Balance			−1.8
Liquid short-term capital	2.3	0.0	
Balance on Official Reserve Account			+0.5
Change in Official Reserves	0.0	0.5	
Balance on Total Account			0.0

cern. For this reason, several different surplus or deficit concepts are used to analyze the balance of payments.

The first surplus or deficit concept is called the balance on *net export account*, and it is a component of aggregate demand. This balance is important because aggregate demand is functionally related to the volume of employment and the level of prices. Unemployment occurs when aggregate demand is deficient, inflation when it is excessive. The balance (B) on net export account, which is exports minus imports ($B = X − M$), equals real income (Y) minus real domestic expenditure (E), which is the total expenditure of consumers, government, and investors ($E = C + G + I$); that is,

$$B = Y − E$$

which is merely another way of writing the GNP equation ($Y = C + G + I + X − M$). The balance (B) can alter aggregate demand and, in turn, can be altered by changes in income (Y) or by changes in real domestic expenditure (E). Income (Y) is generated by the production of exports as well as by the production of goods and services for domestic use; and real domestic expenditure includes consumer, government, and investor purchases of imported goods and services as well as purchases of domestic goods and services. In Table 10–1, there is a deficit of $1.4 billion on net export account.

A second concept of surplus or deficit is called the *basic balance*. The basic balance shows the net position of the balance of payments after including imports and exports, transfers, and long-term capital transactions. These items are basic in the sense that they represent the main reasons for engaging in international trade in the first place. In contrast, short-term capital flows and official foreign exchange transactions, the remaining items, are often viewed as accommodating transactions. They are undertaken to finance the basic transactions. To a certain extent, this distinction between a basic and accommodating transaction is fictitious. For example, long-term financing is sometimes used to accommodate imports or exports. The basic balance in Table 10–1 shows a deficit of $5.1 billion.

Third, the United States uses a liquidity concept to measure its balance of payments deficit. A financial asset is said to be liquid if it can be converted into currency (in this case, U.S. dollars) within a short period of time, usually less than one year. The *liquidity balance* is intended to measure the ability of the United States to defend the dollar, that is, to convert dollars into gold. It includes the change in dollars held by foreigners plus the change in U.S. short-term liabilities to foreigners that can be converted into dollars within a year minus the change in U.S. official reserves (gold plus government-held claims on foreigners). The world monetary crisis of the early 1970s occurred because liquid claims against the United States increased so rapidly that it became apparent that U.S. gold and other reserve assets were inadequate to defend the dollar. As a result, the dollar was declared to be inconvertible.

Finally, the balance on official reserve account shows what has happened to the official reserves of a country. For most countries, official reserves include gold, foreign currencies (mainly U.S. dollars), and the net position with the International Monetary Fund (IMF). The IMF acts as an international central banker in the foreign exchange market by holding deposits and making loans to most non-Communist governments. For the United States, dollars are not a reserve currency because they are not a claim on foreigners. Official reserves were an essential part of the fixed foreign exchange rate system that was established by the Bretton Woods agreement in 1944. Each country was expected to maintain the value of its currency at an official rate in terms of other currencies within a stipulated margin. If market forces pushed the value of a currency up or down, the country was supposed to increase or decrease its official reserves in order to stabilize the value of its currency. Under a completely flexible exchange rate system, reserves would be unnecessary; each currency would fluctuate according to the forces of supply and demand. Following the collapse of the Bretton Woods system, exchange rates have been allowed to float, but governments have used their reserves to prevent them from floating erratically.

Table 10–1 employs some hypothetical figures to show how the various surplus and deficit concepts are related. The balance on net export account shows that imports exceeded exports by $1.4 billion. The basic balance records even a larger deficit, because transfers paid plus long-term capital outflows exceeded transfers received plus long-term capital inflows. The liquidity balance also shows a deficit, but the deficit has been reduced by a net surplus on nonliquid short-term capital account, which would occur, for example, when foreigners pay off short-term loans from residents. Official reserves increased, indicating that the monetary authority acquired foreign exchange (sold domestic currency) in order to hold the value of the domestic currency down to its official rate. The balance on the total account always equals zero.

Why a Surplus or Deficit May Be a Problem

A workable system of international payments is essential to world trade, without which countries could not enjoy the benefits of specialization in production or variety in consumption. American computers, British sports cars, Canadian wheat, French wine, German chemicals, Japanese television sets, and all the other goods sold on world markets would be restricted to their native lands. Laborers and capitalists would not gain the income earned from exports, and consumers could not buy many of the foreign wares that they prefer to domestic products. The economic self-interest of nations prompts them to support and maintain the system of international payments.

A balance-of-payments surplus or deficit is not inherently desirable or undesirable, either from the point of view of one nation or all nations. Neither surpluses nor deficits necessarily inflict a hardship on particular people the way in which unemployment and inflation do, though a surplus of merchandise exports over imports is often regarded as an advantage and is called a "favorable balance of trade." A deficit, however, permits a country to consume more than it produces, which may be even more appealing. Balance-of-payments policy is more often concerned with the impact of a particular surplus or deficit on employment, prices, economic growth, or other domestic problems than it is with the question of whether a particular surplus or deficit is a "good thing" in itself.

Unemployment can be caused by a balance-of-payments deficit on net export account. When imports rise above exports, the aggregate demand for domestic output is reduced below what it would otherwise be. A reduction in output tends to decrease employment and increase unemployment. To the extent that a balance-of-payments deficit contributes to unemployment, that deficit is undesirable and should be avoided.

Inflation can be caused by a surplus of exports over imports. The net export balance (*B*) is the foreign component of aggregate demand; domestic expenditure (*E*) by consumers, government, and investors is the other component. Together (*E* + *B*) they equal output in equilibrium. If the aggregate demand for goods and services is increased beyond the productive capacity of the economy by a net export surplus, prices tend to rise.

Economic growth can be accelerated by international capital flows. Newly developing countries frequently want foreign capital in order to increase their productive capacity. Without capital funds from abroad, they will not be able to finance as much domestic investment in new capital goods as they want. Without foreign funds, either domestic investment must be reduced or domestic saving increased. Greater saving means that consumers must be induced to give up part of their current consumption, which may not be far above subsistence. In order for the balance-of-payments account to be in equilibrium at the level of the basic balance, a capital-importing country must run a deficit on its current account (trade and transfers).

A chronic balance-of-payments disequilibrium may ultimately force a country to depreciate or appreciate its currency. When a country has a basic deficit for a number of years, it tends to run out of official reserves, so that market forces will depreciate its currency if the government does not devalue it first. When a surplus occurs, a country can always increase its official reserves, but reserves can not be increased without limit. Countries that are running deficits may devalue their currencies, which has the effect of appreciating the currency of a country running a surplus. Rather than devalue their own currencies, deficit countries may exert political pressure on a surplus country to appreciate its currency. Finally, a surplus country is in the position of accepting foreign currency in exchange for real goods and services—paper dollars for Volkswagons, for example—something it may not be prepared to do forever.

Currency appreciation or depreciation changes the terms of trade and tends to alter the allocation of resources and the distribution of income. Terms of trade are measured by the ratio of prices received for exports to prices paid for imports. On the one hand, depreciation causes a country to give a larger quantity of exports for a given quantity of imports; its terms of trade worsen. Giving more for less, in itself, is obviously not desirable. On the other hand, appreciation, which permits a country to export less for a given quantity of imports, will tend to reduce output and cause unemployment in export industries and in industries that compete with imports. When the terms of trade change, output and income tend to shift from one industry to another, so that some people benefit at the expense of others.

Political power, rather than economic well-being, may motivate a country to seek a favorable balance of trade and increase its official reserves. If it runs low on reserves, the market alone can force it to adjust its balance of payments at a time and in a manner that it may not want; but if its reserves are ample, it enjoys a large measure of political independence. Its national sovereignty can not so easily be infringed by its trading partners or by the International Monetary Fund. A balance-of-payments adjustment, should it become necessary, can be undertaken gradually and with a considerable degree of flexibility.

Not all countries can run a balance-of-payments surplus at the same time. If one country exports more than it imports, at least one other country must import more than it exports. If national sovereignty prompts all countries to seek a favorable balance of trade, a trade war will ensue, the whole system of international payments will be weakened, and nearly everyone will lose. Both peace and prosperity will be undermined.

Policy Tools

A balance-of-payments disequilibrium becomes a policy issue when it is substantial and persistent. Under a fixed exchange rate system, minor fluctuations in international reserves about a safe level occur all the time and do not require corrective policies. However, a fundamental disequilibrium, one which is substantial and persistent, may ultimately require the government to pursue policies that change the volume or the composition of aggregate demand.

The balance of exports minus imports (B) can be altered by changing income (Y), which equals domestic expenditures (E) plus net exports (B), or by changing the division of total expenditure between foreign and domestic products. Fiscal policy is primarily an income changing policy, which affects the balance of net exports by its influence on imports. Monetary policy is also an income changing policy; but, in addition, it affects net capital flows by its influence on interest rates. Exchange rate policy tends to switch expenditures between foreign and domestic products by changing the terms of trade. Selective controls that restrict imports or expand exports alter the composition of aggregate demand and are classified as expenditure-switching policies.[1]

Fiscal policy governs the amount of government purchases, transfer payments, and taxes (see Chapter 5). An expansionary fiscal policy tends to increase the level of income by increasing purchases or transfers or by decreasing taxes; a restrictive policy does the opposite. Since imports vary directly with income, an expansionary policy tends to reduce net exports, while a restrictive policy tends to produce a net export surplus. Thus, fiscal policy can be used to correct a balance-of-payments disequilibrium, though at the same time it will tend to create either inflation or unemployment.

Monetary policy (see Chapter 7) determines the quantity of money in circulation and, thereby, affects the rate of interest. The interest rate influences the balance of payments in two reinforcing ways: first, by making domestic investment in new capital goods more or less profitable, it tends to change the level of income and imports; second, by changing the ratio of domestic to foreign interest rates, it alters international capital flows. A tight money policy tends to increase net exports by reducing income and imports, and it also tends to attract capital funds from abroad. An easy money policy does the opposite; it tends to produce a deficit on net export account as well as a deficit on capital account. Because of its influence on interest rates, monetary policy has become the first line of defense against a balance-of-payments disequilibrium.

If a government faces a balance-of-payments deficit and unemployment at the same time, it may pursue a tight money policy that raises interest rates in order to attract funds from abroad and also pursue an expansionary fiscal policy in order to increase income and employment. An expansionary fiscal policy of sufficient strength can be used to counteract the adverse effect of high interest rates on investment and income, so that output is increased to the full employment level. The high interest rates also tend to balance the deficit on net export account with a surplus on capital account. Thus, both full employment and a balance-of-payments equilibrium obtain. However, high interest

---

[1] The distinction between an expenditure increasing (decreasing) policy and an expenditure switching policy was generalized by H. G. Johnson, "Towards a General Theory of the Balance of Payments," in R. E. Caves and H. G. Johnson (eds.), *A.E.A. Readings in International Economics* (Homewood, Ill.: Richard D. Irwin, 1968).

rates at home will tend to retard capital accumulation and economic growth, so that it may be better to alter the official exchange rate or to use selective controls on imports and exports.

Exchange rate policy affects the price that residents must pay for foreign currencies in order to buy imports and the price that foreigners must pay for the domestic currency in order to buy exports. Provided that the demand for imports and exports is sufficiently elastic, a devaluation (official depreciation) will tend to eliminate a balance-of-payments deficit, and a revaluation (official appreciation) will tend to eliminate a surplus (see Chapter 6). When a demand curve is sufficiently elastic, the percentage change in the quantity demanded exceeds the percentage change in price, so that a fall in price increases the dollar volume of sales (price times quantity) and vice versa for a rise in price. Thus, a currency depreciation, which reduces the foreign price of exports and increases the domestic price of imports, tends to increase the value of exports, decrease the value of imports, and produce a surplus on net export account. Appreciation reverses this sequence.

Until the early 1970s, the exchange rate was used infrequently as a policy tool, because under the Bretton Woods system countries agreed to maintain fixed exchange rates unless they had a "fundamental" balance-of-payments disequilibrium, in which case a single abrupt change was permitted. Milton Friedman[2] of the University of Chicago and many other academic economists favor adoption of a flexible exchange rate system in which the free market forces of supply and demand will tend to keep the balance of payments in equilibrium (see Chapter 6). However, central banks and national governments prefer to work with officially fixed exchange rates for several reasons.

First, an international agreement is necessary for any system to work. One country does not have the power to change its exchange rate without the implicit or explicit agreement of other countries. Other countries can always retaliate. During the 1930s, countries with high rates of unemployment depreciated their currencies in order to increase aggregate demand and reduce unemployment. This led to retaliation and exchange rate wars.

Second, national governments are responsible for maintaining full employment and price stability and for promoting economic growth, which they usually regard as more important policy objectives than an equilibrium in their balance of

---

[2] Milton Friedman, "The Case for Flexible Exchange Rates," *Essays in Positive Economics* (Chicago: University of Chicago Press, 1953), pp. 157–203.

payments. Since a country's exchange rate can have a substantial effect on domestic output, employment, and prices, a government has a strong incentive for using its exchange rate to improve the performance of its own economy. A perfectly working flexible exchange rate system that maintains the balance of payments in equilibrium not only requires a government to sacrifice a useful tool for controlling its domestic economy but also elevates the objective of equilibrium in the balance of payments above the objectives of full employment, price stability, and economic growth. Japan, among other countries, deliberately undervalues its currency in order to stimulate economic growth in its export industries.

Third, even if the major industrial countries did agree to a flexible exchange rate system and did not intervene in the foreign exchange rate market, speculators might try to manipulate exchange rates to their profit. Given the size of the currency holdings of the Bank of America or the Sheik of Kuwait, such speculation could cause wild fluctuations in exchange rates and could, thereby, adversely affect the economies of many countries.

Fourth, floating, or flexible, exchange rates make international transactions more uncertain than fixed exchange rates. No one knows for sure how much must be paid for imports or how much will be received for exports until the exchange rate is known. This difficulty can be overcome by the forward exchange market, where foreign currency can be bought or sold today for delivery in the future. For example, an American importer who orders $250,000 worth of British goods today could at the same time buy £100,000 at $2.50 a pound in order to pay for his goods when they are delivered.

Before the collapse of the Bretton Woods agreement, Canada had experimented with a system that is between the officially fixed and the freely floating systems. It used a *controlled float*; that is, it let its currency float, but it used its reserves to make sure that it did not float too far in either direction. At the time, the United States called this a "dirty float" because it permitted Canada to manipulate its exchange rate to its own advantage.

After the collapse of the Bretton Woods agreement, most countries were forced to adopt the Canadian system and use a controlled float. It combines the advantages of both the fixed and the flexible systems. Like the fixed system, it can be used to stabilize exchange rates in the short run to provide certainty and facilitate trade; and it can be used to discourage speculation by pitting the central bank against the speculator. Like the flexible system, it permits exchange rates to adjust gradually over time in response to fundamental changes, instead of changing abruptly as occurred under the Bretton Woods system. However, it has one major fault: without an agreement on variations in exchange rates, it risks an exchange rate war like the one that occurred in the 1930s.

Selective controls include all those policies that alter the way in which the market allocates imports, exports, and capital. Sometimes they are obvious, as in the following cases: a *tariff* is a tax on imports, a *quota* or *embargo* imposes limits on the quantities of imports, *exchange controls* restrict access to foreign currency, and a *subsidy* increases the profitability of export industries. Sometimes these controls are hidden in health regulations, electrical standards, corporation tax laws, and so on. Their effect is to switch expenditures from foreign to domestic products.

The United States used a variety of selective controls during the 1960s and early 1970s. It limited the amount of duty-free goods that tourists could bring home; it taxed certain types of capital outflows with the so-called Interest Equalization Tax; it imposed a temporary surcharge on imports; it allowed domestic corporations to avoid profit taxes on export sales; and so on. Direct controls can be effective, and, as temporary measures, they probably do little harm. However, they tend to become permanent and to reduce efficiency as high-cost domestic goods are substituted for low-cost foreign goods. They also invite retaliation.

Internal and External Balance

Full employment, stable prices, and equilibrium in the balance of payments are three main goals of economic policy. In this section, full employment without inflation is referred to as an internal balance, which occurs when neither an inflationary gap nor a deflationary gap exists between the aggregate demand and the productive capacity of the economy. An external balance means equilibrium in the balance of payments, which occurs when neither an excess supply nor an excess demand exists in the foreign exchange market.

When an internal balance and an external balance do not exist simultaneously, the government faces a dilemma that is similar to the dilemma of inflation with unemployment, which was discussed in Chapter 9. Policy measures that alleviate one problem often aggravate the other. This is illustrated in Figure

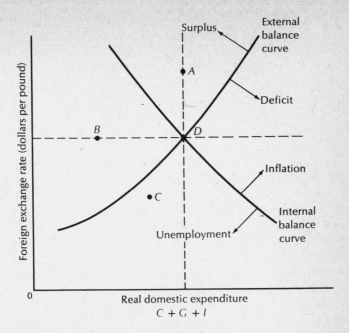

Figure 10-1 **Internal and External Balance**

10–1, which is adapted from a diagram by T. W. Swan,[3] an Australian economist.

Real domestic expenditure (*E*) in constant dollars appears on the horizontal axis. It is the sum of consumer expenditures (*C*), government purchases (*G*), and investment in newly produced capital goods (*I*). Each of these components could include imported goods and services. Since real domestic expenditure excludes the net export (*B*) component of aggregate demand, it can increase without changing the level of aggregate demand provided the net export balance decreases dollar for dollar. For example, if the full employment level of output is $100 billion, real domestic expenditure could rise to $110 billion, provided net exports fell to a negative $10 billion, that is, provided imports exceeded exports by $10 billion.

The foreign exchange rate appears on the vertical axis.[4] It measures the price of pounds in terms of dollars (dollars

---

[3] T. W. Swan, "Longer-run Problems of the Balance of Payment," in R. E. Caves and H. G. Johnson (eds.), *A.E.A. Readings in International Economics* (Homewood, Ill.: Richard D. Irwin, 1968).

[4] Instead of the foreign exchange rate, any other policy that switches expenditures between foreign and domestic products could be measured along the vertical axis.

per pound) and assumes that the dollar is the domestic currency and the pound is the foreign currency, as in Figure 6–3. Movements up the vertical axis occur as the dollar depreciates, that is, as it takes more dollars to buy a pound; movements down reflect appreciation of the dollar, that is, fewer dollars buy a pound. Provided the demand for imports and exports is sufficiently elastic, depreciation increases the net export balance (B) and, thereby, increases aggregate demand. Appreciation reduces net exports and aggregate demand.

The internal balance curve reflects the constant level of real income that is necessary to maintain full employment without inflation. It slopes downward to the right, because net exports must decline as real domestic expenditure rises. Net exports decline as the dollar appreciates (that is, as the exchange rate moves down the vertical axis). Suppose the economy is at point D. If the government pursues an expansionary fiscal policy by increasing government purchases (G), inflation will tend to occur, unless net exports fall enough to offset the expansionary fiscal policy. If the economy is at point D and the government reduces spending, unemployment will tend to occur. Thus, inflation occurs above and unemployment below the internal balance curve.

The external balance curve shows what must happen to the foreign exchange rate and real domestic expenditure in order to maintain the balance of payments in equilibrium. When real domestic expenditure increases, income tends to rise; and, since imports are directly related to income, imports rise, too. Given the level of exports, therefore, an increase in real domestic expenditure tends to produce a balance-of-payments deficit. However, if the dollar depreciates, which is shown by an upward movement along the vertical axis, net exports will tend to rise. Domestic products become cheaper for foreigners to purchase at the same time that imports become more expensive. The external balance curve shows how much the dollar must depreciate to maintain the balance of payments in equilibrium as real domestic expenditure rises.

Suppose that the economy is at point D. If real domestic expenditure increases while the exchange rate is unchanged, imports rise and a deficit on net export account develops. A reduction of real domestic expenditure would produce a surplus, by the same reasoning. Starting at point D again, if the dollar depreciates while real domestic expenditure is unchanged, a surplus of exports over imports will arise. An appreciation would produce a deficit under the same condition. Thus, a balance-of-payments deficit occurs below the external balance line, a surplus above it.

The internal balance and external balance curves divide Figure 10–1 into "four zones of economic unhappiness." North of both curves, inflation and a balance-of-payments surplus occur; to the west, there is unemployment and a surplus; to the south, unemployment and a deficit; and to the east, inflation and a deficit. Only at point *D* is there full employment, stable prices, and an equilibrium in the balance of payments.

Macroeconomic policy should direct the economy toward a position of internal and external balance by moving toward point *D*. If the economy is on the vertical dotted line, say at point *A*, the balance-of-payments surplus and the inflation can be eliminated merely by revaluing the dollar. An appreciation of the currency tends to reduce net exports and, thereby, reduce the balance-of-payments surplus. The reduction of net exports also diminishes aggregate demand and tends to eliminate the inflationary gap. When West Germany appreciated its currency in the early 1970s, it tended to reduce its balance-of-payments surplus and its domestic inflation at the same time. Similarly, if the economy is on the horizontal dotted line, say at *B*, the balance-of-payments surplus and the unemployment can be reduced by an expansionary fiscal policy alone. If government purchases are increased, for example, income will rise and tend to reduce the unemployment. At the same time, as income rises, imports will increase and tend to reduce the balance-of-payments surplus.

A single economic policy is not sufficient to correct two different problems in most cases. If the economy is at point *C* in Figure 10–1, an expansionary fiscal policy can be used to eliminate the unemployment; but, as the economy moves horizontally toward the internal balance curve, the balance-of-payments deficit will worsen. Thus, a second policy, such as a currency depreciation, is needed to deal with the balance-of-payments deficit. Unless the economy happens to be on the dotted lines, two policies are needed: one to change the level of income and another to switch expenditures between foreign and domestic products.

Unemployment, inflation, and a balance-of-payments disequilibrium can all exist at the same time, which further complicates macroeconomic policy. Jan Tinbergen, the Dutch Nobel Prize winner in economics, once noted that a government needs at least as many policy tools as the number of problems to be solved.[5] But that is not all. Even if a government faced a single problem, a single corrective policy would often be insufficient. Whatever the corrective tool, it is likely to stir up other problems in its wake. Fiscal policy, monetary policy, exchange rate policy, incomes policy, and selective controls all affect employment, prices, the balance of payments, the allocation of resources, and so on. Using an expansionary monetary or fiscal policy to combat unemployment will tend to cause inflation and a balance-of-payments deficit. Using an exchange rate depreciation to combat a balance-of-payments deficit will increase aggregate demand, raise import prices, and tend to cause inflation. Incomes policy and selective controls tend to misallocate resources. Thus, whether a government faces one problem or many problems, it must be prepared to use a combination of corrective policies.

---

[5] Jan Tinbergen, *On the Theory of Economic Policy* (Amsterdam: North-Holland Press, 1952).

INDEX

About the Author

PETER C. DOOLEY is presently Associate Professor of Economics and Political Science at the University of Saskatchewan. Professor Dooley acquired his Ph.D. at Cornell University in 1964, specializing in economic theory and its history. He is the author of *Elementary Price Theory* and has had articles published in the *American Economic Review* and other journals.

9872